Dead Precedents

# DEAD PRECEDENTS

## How Hip-Hop Defines the Future

**Roy Christopher**

781.649
Christopher
2019

Published by Repeater Books
An imprint of Watkins Media Ltd

Unit 11 Shepperton House
89-93 Shepperton Road
London
N1 3DF
United Kingdom
www.repeaterbooks.com
A Repeater Books paperback original 2019
1

Distributed in the United States by Random House, Inc., New York.

Cover design: Johnny Bull
Typography and typesetting: Frederik Jehle
Typefaces: Meriden LT Std, Arial

ISBN: 9781912248346
Ebook ISBN: 9781912248353

Printed and bound in the United Kingdom by TJ International Ltd

In memoriam,

Hsi-Chang Lin
Mark Fisher
Sean Price


r.i.P!

# CONTENTS

*All ways lead west, beyond the earth's frontiers,*
*And tides race outward-bound, beyond the sun,*
*To ride the shining coasts of distant spheres.*
*See where the cloud-caught airy currents run?*

*Oceans and islands call! Far and beyond*
*Extends the timeless challenge, star by star*
*Down paths of light, part guerdon and part bond,*
*To pull us westward, lifting sail and spar.*

*O pioneers, this earth, this island shore*
*Is but mid-passage in the enterprise —*
*One dream, one port where cockleshell and oar*
*Might know the deeps that border deeper skies,*

*To live our earth-bound infancy of eons to rehearse*
*The casting off — the voyage towards universe.*

— Raymond R. Patterson, *26 Ways of Looking at a Black Man*

# PREFACE

"Space, that endless series of speculations and origins — of rebirths and electric spankings — is here not so much a metaphor as it is a series of fragmented selves, a place of possibilities and debris and explorations and atmosphere."
— Kevin Young, *The Grey Album: On the Blackness of Blackness*

"Let us imagine these hip-hop principles as a blueprint for social resistance and affirmation: create sustaining narratives, accumulate them, layer, embellish, and transform them."
— Tricia Rose, *Black Noise: Rap Music and Black Culture in Contemporary America*

Several years ago, on one of my online profiles under "books" I listed only Donald Goines and Philip K. Dick. If you don't know them, Donald Goines wrote about himself and his associates and their struggles as street hustlers, pimps, players, and dopefiends. Philip K. Dick wrote about the brittleness of reality, its wavy, funhouse perceptions through drugs and dreams. Goines wrote sixteen books in five years and Dick wrote forty-four in thirty. Both were heavy users of mind-altering substances (heroin and amphetamines, respectively), and both helped redefine the genres in which they wrote. They interrogated the nature of human identity, one through the inner city and the other through inner space.

While I am certainly a fan of both authors, I posted them together on my profile as kind of a gag. I thought their juxtaposition was weird enough to spark questions if you were familiar with their work, and if you weren't, it wouldn't matter. I had no idea that I would be writing about the overlapping layers of their legacies so many years later.

To retrofit a description, one could say that Goines' books are gangster-rap literature. They're referenced in rap songs by everyone from Tupac and Ice-T to Ludacris and Nas. In many instances, Dick's work could be called proto-cyberpunk. The Philip K. Dick Award was launched the year after he died, and two of the first three were awarded to the premiere novels of cyberpunk: *Software* by Rudy Rucker in 1983 and *Neuromancer* by William Gibson in 1985.

When cyberpunk and hip-hop were both entering their Golden Age, I was in high school. One day I was walking up my friend Thomas Durdin's driveway. By the volume of the AC/DC sample that forms the backbone of Boogie Down Productions' "Dope Beat," I knew his mom wasn't home. Along with the decibel level, I was also struck by how the uncanny pairing of Australian hard rock and New York street slang sounded. It was gritty. It was brash. It rocked. De La Soul's 1996 record, *Stakes is High*, opens with the question, "Where were you when you first heard *Criminal Minded*?" That moment was a door opening to a new world.

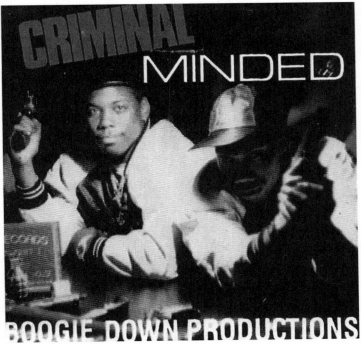

The Blueprint: *Criminal Minded*.

I didn't realize it then, but that new world was the twenty-first century, and hip-hop was its blueprint.

I distinctly remember that the label on the record spinning around on Thomas's turntable incorrectly named the song "Hope Beats." An interesting mistake given that DJ Scott La Rock was killed just months after the record came out, prompting KRS-One to start the Stop the Violence movement. Where *Criminal Minded* is often cited as a forerunner of gangster rap, KRS-One was thereafter dedicated to peace. I'd heard hip-hop before, but the unfamiliar familiarity of the "Back in Black" guitar samples in that song make that particular day stick in my head.

Long before hip-hop went digital, mixtapes — those floppy discs of the boombox and car stereo — facilitated the spread of underground music. The first time I heard hip-hop, it was on such a tape. Hiss and pop were as much a part of the experience of those mixes as the scratching and rapping. We didn't even know what to call it, but we stayed up late to listen. We copied and traded those tapes until they were barely listenable. As soon as I figured out how, I started making my own. We watched hip-hop go from those scratchy mixtapes to compact discs to shiny-suit videos on MTV, from Fab 5 Freddy to Public Enemy to P. Diddy, from Run-DMC to N.W.A. to Notorious B.I.G. Others lost interest along the way. I never did.

A lot of people all over the world heard those early tapes and were impacted as well. Having spread from New York City to parts unknown, hip-hop became a global phenomenon. Every school has aspiring emcees, rapping to beats banged out on lunchroom tables. Every city has kids rhyming on the corner, trying to outdo each other with adept attacks and clever comebacks. The cipher circles the planet. In a lot of other places, hip-hop culture *is* American culture.

Though their roots go back much further, the subcultures of hip-hop and cyberpunk emerged in the mass mind during the 1980s. Sometimes they're both self-consciously of the era, but digging through their artifacts and narratives, we will see the seeds of our times sprouting. We will view hip-hop not only as a genre of music and a vibrant subculture but also as a set of cultural practices that transcend both of those. We will explore cyberpunk not only as a subgenre of science fiction but also as the rise of computer culture, the tectonic shifting of all things to digital forms and formats, and the making and hacking thereof. If we take hip-hop as a community of practice, then its cultural practices inform the new century in new ways. "I didn't see a subculture," Rammellzee once said, "I saw a culture in development."

The subtitle of this book could just as easily be "How Hip-Hop *Defies* the Future." As one of hip-hop culture's pioneers, Grandmaster Caz, is fond of saying, "Hip-hop didn't invent anything. Hip-hop reinvented *everything*." To establish this foundation, we will start with a few views of hip-hop culture (Endangered Theses), followed by a brief look at the origins of cyberpunk and hip-hop (Margin Prophets). We will then look at four specific areas of hip-hop music: recording, archiving, sampling, and intertextuality (Fruit of the Loot); the appropriating of pop culture and hacking of language (Spoken Windows); and graffiti and other visual aspects of the culture (The Process of Illumination). From there we will go ghost hunting through the willful haunting of hip-hop and cyberculture (Let Bygones Be Icons). All of this in the service of remapping hip-hop's spread from around the way to around the world and what that means for the culture of the now and the future (Return to Cinder).

The aim of this book is to illustrate how hip-hop culture defines twenty-first-century culture. With its infinitely recombinant and revisable history, the music represents futures without pasts. The heroes of this book are the architects of those futures: emcees, DJs, poets, artists, writers. If they didn't invent anything but reinvented everything, then that everything is where we live now. Forget what you know about time and causation. This is a new fossil record with all new futures.

Delicious Demon: Tricky. Photo by Timothy Saccenti.

## Chapter One

# ENDANGERED THESES

"The only important elements in any society are the artistic and the criminal, because they alone, by questioning the society's values, can force it to change."
— Oscar the Lump, in Samuel R. Delany's *Empire Star*

"Tricky's *Maxinquaye* is a kind of ruins of the 80s pop sound. Fragments of Trevor Horn are here, shards of Grace Jones are over there, and tremors of The Bomb Squad are felt everywhere — indeed, 'this is the Aftermath.' One can also read *Maxinquaye* as a kind of electronic mirror erected not towards the future but the past, the last world. The image we see on the CD is that of the 20$^{th}$ century setting behind the landscape of the 80s. We also see that Great Britain's 80s was the most dreamy time-place in the world, for it was muffled by a double twilight: a twilight that was in part its own long decline from the height of the 19$^{th}$ century (this part of the twilight was deepened by the Falklands War which took place 'out... on the perimeter'), and also the end of the Cold War, in which it had a considerable stake and say in the form of Margaret Thatcher. Indeed, Inglan was like a sci-fi planet on whose horizon set two spent suns."
— Charles Mudede, "Twilight of the Goodtimes"

*Maxinquaye* seems perfectly perched on the cusp of so many things, the past and the future piled to a peak underneath, a nodal point obscured by its sheer, shifting beauty. Tricky and his muse, Martina Topley-Bird, blatantly blunted on love and lust, ran aground just as hip-hop was displacing heavy metal as the top-selling musical genre. The so-called "alternative revolution" was well underway, yet Guns N' Roses was all over MTV with opulent, twelve-minute videos and all over the charts with an epic double-disc called *Use Your Illusion*. The music world was wild at heart and weird on top. Underneath that odd veneer of mainstream schizophrenia, subgenres were splitting and dividing like brain-tumor cells. Enabled by recording and sampling technologies that eroded any semblance of cultural cohesion, forecasts of the future and pieces of the past were mixing into an unrecognizable new era.

When something is described as retrospective and futuristic at the same time, we are reminded of how slipshod the present moment truly is. According to accounts by Tricky himself, the name "Maxinquaye" is a combination of Maxine and Quaye, his mother's first and last names. He has also said that the last refers to the Quaye tribe from Africa. Simon Reynolds imagines it as a sort of place name: "the lost Motherland." Tricky's mother committed suicide when he was but an infant, and he sensed her presence in the recording of *Maxinquaye*. "I found out later that she used to write words, poetry, but never showed them to anybody," he says. Whether named after a lost Motherland or a lost mother, the recording endures the double consciousness of the African Diaspora. Though not exclusive to the United States, *double consciousness* is W.E.B. Du Bois's term for the

African-American status of being *in* but not *of* America, "this sense of always looking at one's self through the eyes of others." So prevalent to have become an Afrofuturist cliché, the divide still stands.

Released dead in the middle of the 1990s, Tricky's debut document arrived on the divide of hip-hop history into two eras: from its birth in the mid-1970s up to the deaths of Tupac Shakur and Biggie Smalls in 1996 and 1997 respectively, and the decades since. As big as it was by the mid-1990s, hip-hop had become codified at least twice over, and cyberculture via the web was starting to take hold outside of businesses and institutions. What if Mudede's two suns in the epigraph above were rising on the Western world instead of setting? And what if those two suns were hip-hop and cyberpunk?

"It has become increasingly clear that 1979-80 [...] was a threshold moment," Mark Fisher wrote in *Ghosts of My Life*, "the time when a whole world (social democratic, Fordist, industrial) became obsolete, and the contours of a new world (neoliberal, consumerist, informatic) began to show themselves." Punk was giving way to post-punk, new wave, goth, and hip-hop. The Cold War hung heavy and cocaine was sprinkled throughout creative culture. In very general terms, different drugs inspire different music and different appreciations thereof: think of the shift from marijuana-inspired reggae, prog, and classic rock to coked-out punk, post-punk, and new wave. It's an oversimplification, but those times were different than what came before them. "Any old stupor will do," Reynolds writes of *Maxinquaye*. The 1980s sported a sharper, shinier edge. "Fragments of Trevor Horn are here, shards of Grace Jones are over there, and tremors of The Bomb Squad are felt everywhere," Mudede's words also summarize the decade's soundtrack. These are the sounds of what Svetlana Boym calls *diasporic intimacy*: "Diasporic intimacy is haunted by the images of home and homeland, yet it also discloses some of the furtive pleasures of exile." Like Du Bois's double consciousness, diasporic intimacy is a "shared longing without belonging." It's that feeling when where you're from is at odds with where you're at.

## False Media

Scholars, researchers, and journalists have always had a tumultuous relationship with hip-hop. When hip-hop is taken seriously enough by scholars to write about critically, they quickly point out its obvious negative traits: its violence, vulgar language, misogyny, and heteronormativity. This is akin to going back in time and pointing out racism, sexism, or lower prices. While it's true, it's not exactly news or insightful critique. When hip-hop is taken seriously enough by scholars to write about favorably, they quickly show that they're coming to it from outside the culture, attributing lyrical quotations to Grandmaster Flash when he's the DJ of the group and therefore doesn't speak on their records. This is akin to quoting Echo of Echo & the Bunnymen when "Echo" was the name they gave their drum machine, or Hootie of Hootie & the Blowfish when "Hootie" is not only not the singer, he isn't a member of the band.

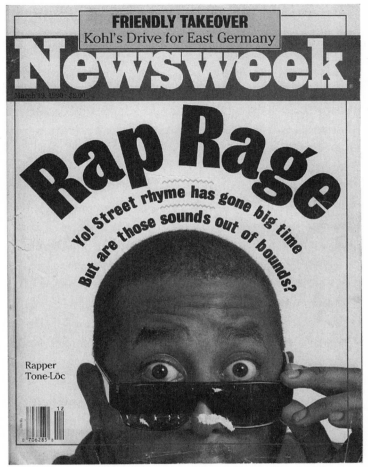

Rap Rage: *Newsweek,* March 19, 1990.

In the March 19, 1990 issue of *Newsweek,* the editors attack hip-hop with everything from unfettered racism to ignorant fear-mongering. In March 1990, rap music was still the bane of popular culture. *Yo! MTV Raps* had barely started its decade-long run, N.W.A. had yet to release records from their separate ways, Public Enemy was on the verge of dropping *Fear of a Black Planet*, and Tipper Gore's Parents Music Resource Center was advising parents not to let their kids listen to rap. In *Newsweek*'s cover story, "Rap Rage," with the cover copy, "Yo! Street rhyme has gone big time, but are those sounds out of bounds?" Jerry Adler attempts to describe music made by groups "most Americans may never have heard of,"

> [...] music so postindustrial it's almost not even played, but pieced together out of prerecorded sound bites. It is the culture of American males frozen in various stages of adolescence: their streetwise music, their ugly macho boasting and joking about anyone who hangs out on a different block — cops, other races, women, and homosexuals.

Hip-hop journalist Bill Adler (no relation) writes of the cover story,

> It was so off-base that 49 music writers, led by *Entertainment Weekly*'s Greg Sandow (and representing publications including *Time*, *USA Today*, *The Los Angeles Times*, *The Washington Post*, *Rolling Stone*, and *The Village Voice*) wrote a letter to the editors of *Newsweek* insisting that [Jerry] Adler had "invented a nightmarish and racist fantasy about ignorant Black men who scream obscene threats." This is more than artistic misjudgment. Adler has slandered a major strain of contemporary Black culture.

This attitude persists over two decades later, in the October 18, 2012 issue of the *Chicago Sun-Times*, for example. Furthering Chicago's Chief Keef as an ephemeral media lightning rod, all the bias, misinformation, and well-worn themes from the history of mainstream hip-hop coverage are here, from jail time boosting record sales to record companies exploiting violence. I call Keef's treatment ephemeral because comparing him to Tupac and T.I. — as Thomas Conner does in this article — is ludicrous and illustrates how little these writers know about their subject matter or care about reporting it accurately.

Keef is a known associate of the Black Disciples gang. These gangs use coded language to dis each other in rap songs and videos online. Keef is down with the Lamon faction of the Black Disciples, whose rivalry with the Gangster Disciples goes back to the 1970s. Keef regularly uses the number "300" in his songs, a reference to his affiliation. In May 2012, one of Keef's rivals, Lil Jojo, posted a song called "3hunnak," meaning "300 killer." The song was rapped over the instrumental of the Chief Keef song "Everyday." Lil Jojo replaced the "every day" of the chorus with "BDK," meaning Black Disciples killer. Jojo's aunt claims he was trying to do a "Tupac and Biggie thing [to] get under the skin of" Keef and his people. His mother adds, "They were feuding in the rap game." Lil Jojo was killed on September 4, 2012. A few months later, as he was sentenced on probation violation charges for handling and firing a gun in a video, Chief Keef had the eighth-best-selling rap record in the country.

Chief Keef at Lollapalooza, 2012.
Photo by Mary Beeze.

Keef popularized a rap style called "drill music" that originated in Chicago's South Side. Its use of truncated half-bars made up of single statements chanted one at a time rather than rap's signature flowing poetry over beats makes it a distinctive vocal expression, possibly only prefigured by other one-offs like early-1990s dis-rapper Tim Dog from New York or the hoarse-voiced Mystikal of New Orleans. It's a style that other rappers sound cramped attempting to emulate, as proven by Kanye West's remix of Keef's first hit "I Don't Like," featuring the ample vocal skills of Pusha-T, Jadakiss, Big Sean, and West himself — all veterans compared to the seventeen-year-old Keef. "Mr. West has rarely sounded so out of place," writes Jon Caramanica, "and the original trumps the remix in every regard. 'I Don't Like' is all hard angles and concrete walls, resistant to whatever nuance Mr. West wanted to add." The drill sound's closest contemporary analogue lies in the gang-fuss, club anthems of Atlanta's Waka Flocka Flame, which feature a little more in the way of flow but are no less clipped and shouted. He's already outlasted his critics' expectations though, and has made the transition from street tough to entertainer with a sort of gangster's grace. That shift still remains for Keef.

Unlike the other writers mentioned here, I like Chief Keef, but I can't say that I hear evidence of a talent like Tupac, T.I., or, more germanely, Tyler, The Creator. Mark Brown opens his *Chicago Sun-Times* article about record labels exploiting violence, such as the gun waving seen in Keef's video, by writing, "There probably ought to be a rule against a guy like me writing about somebody like teen rapper Chief Keef, the gulf between our worlds so vast that there's no way I can relate to his life experiences let alone his music." He adds later, "I decided long ago there's no value in old white guys wagging their fingers about the dangers of rap music lyrics that glorify guns, drugs, violence, and other criminal activity. I don't like them. So what?" One wonders then why he spent nearly eight-hundred words doing just that.

Chief Keef's raps are like Tweets: one-line, stand-alone missives; all comment, no story. Another *Sun-Times* article from 2012 revisits how social media fuels public feuds. Much has been written about the role Twitter played in Keef's rise to infamy, mainly due to gang rivalries that bubbled up into the music and possibly resulted in the death of his South-Side rap rival Lil Jojo. "THE defining document of hip-hop's current evolutionary state isn't a song, or a music video or a concert," writes Caramanica, "Years from now cultural archaeologists will do much better to look back over the Twitter account of the 17-year-old Chicago rapper Chief Keef, who's been exploding, or imploding, depending on how you look at it, one short burst of text at a time." The immediacy of such a channel lends it to hotheaded responses and often eventual regret. "I think it's pretty likely that instantaneity means there is no chance to 'count to 10' in hopes that things might cool off a bit," says my colleague at the University of Illinois-Chicago, Steve Jones, who's quoted in the *Sun-Times* article. He adds, "If Facebook is a wall, Twitter might be a bullhorn."

The bullhorn is the perfect symbol for the incessant blurting of social media and maybe for the more in-your-face aspects of rap itself. It's a more apt symbol than most writers use. One of the core arguments of this book is that hip-hop is inherently futuristic. As illustrated above, many outright reject the future it represents. Some, seemingly refusing to contend with hip-hop's deep roots at all, trace its cultural practices of appropriation, sampling, and remixing back to the collages of the Dadaists, the *détournements* of the Situationists, or the cut-ups of William Burroughs and Brion Gysin. Regardless, there's no denying that hip-hop brought sampling, scratching, and manipulating previously recorded sounds to a global audience. Technologically enabled cutting and pasting are now preeminent practices not only for musicians but also filmmakers, designers, storytellers — culture creators of all kinds.

I bring up these critiques of myopic music journalists and media scholars not just to make fun but to show what hip-hop culture is up against, to show how the dominant culture approaches it, and to show how hip-hop handles them. In African-American traditions, a cut-and-pasted appropriation, what Henry Louis Gates, Jr. describes as "repetition *with a difference*" is called "signifyin'." The practice can be found in every African-American music, from jazz and blues, where riffs, tempos, phrasings, and key changes are cut-up and varied, to hip-hop, where samples and lyrics are looped, repeated, interpolated. The cultural practice of signifyin' alludes to the dross of the dominant culture — slogans, headlines, names, jingles, and so on — as texts against which to mark such a difference, as codes and signs to hack, as meanings to hijack. Trespassing on mainstream metaphors, appropriating the language of those in power is a significant act of individual resistance.

As we will see, the twenty-first century's re-pasting of the past yields a culture that's contextually lossy and thoroughly haunted by reanimated memories. Thanks to recording technology, we live in an era where the past mingles with the present in manners unavailable in earlier times. Being made up of past bits of recorded music, hip-hop is willfully unmoored from the flow of time. The singularity of making recordings out of other recordings is neither a rapture we can return from nor a rupture we can repair. It's a break with the natural order, a repurposing of the past for all new futures.

As Tricky says, "Brand new, you're retro."

Hip-Hop Hacker: Grandmaster Flash. Image by Gary Williams.

## Chapter Two

# MARGIN PROPHETS

"We are the hackers of abstraction. We produce new concepts, new perceptions, new sensations, hacked out of raw data. Whatever code we hack, be it programming language, poetic language, math or music, curves or colorings, we are the abstracters of new worlds."
— McKenzie Wark, *A Hacker Manifesto*

"So what is punk? It's primitive lizard-brain passion clawing its way through the cerebrum of urbanity. The emotive electric acidjuice of adolescence decoding the palimpsest of civilization, stripping it away to expose deeper codes. Graffiti painting its postliterate mark on the official billboards. It's the re-assertion and re-adaptation of the genetic code over the industrial one that has tried to oppress it. It's the war between natural and artificial, and their inevitable deconstruction, their collapse into each other as meaningless distinctions."
— David Porush, "Frothing in the Synaptic Bath"

"You'll never represent my intention. You need more than a mic and a mention."
—Tricky, "Brand New You're Retro"

Looking at images from hip-hop's early days feels like peering into the future. The decimated post-apocalyptic scene of the South Bronx, the repurposing of outmoded recording technology, wild-style screen-names on every colorfast surface, the gloves, the goggles, the gyrating moves: an entire culture cobbled together from the fragments of past fads and fashions. Add the leather-clad mohawks of Afrika Bambaataa and the Soulsonic Force or Rammellzee's B-boy battle armor and one might think they were picking up the pieces after a complete global meltdown. It's a glimpse of a possible future, and that's not to mention the way it sounds when a booming breakbeat clashes perfectly with just the right horn stab or guitar riff, or when Professor Griff barks, "Armageddon has been in effect! Go get a late pass!" Cultural critic Mark Dery says of those early days,

> I came to understand hip-hop as black cyberpunk, a form of techno-bricolage, reading it through William Gibson's canonical formulation ("the street finds its own uses for things") — an appropriation of Levi-Strauss's *bricoleur*, updated for the age of wheels of steel amid the bombed-out urban ruins brought to you by Robert Moses and decades of "benign neglect."

With its burnt-out buildings and broken windows, the South Bronx became an emblem of urban erasure, a wound of highway-bound white flight. It was late-night monologue fodder, a cautionary movie set, and a political pawn piece. Upon visiting the neighborhood on August 5, 1980, then-President Ronald Reagan commented that it looked like it had been hit by an atomic bomb.

In 2014, Erika M. Anderson, who records under the name EMA, wrote an essay titled, "2014: The Year That Cyberpunk Broke." Her contention was that since the predictions of the cyberpunks had come true, we need their help negotiating the age they saw coming. "In the cyberpunk future," she writes, "shadowy multi-national corporations trafficked in big data, humans often augmented themselves with wearable tech and there was a massive wealth gap between the rich and the poor. Sound familiar?" Most of the O.G. cyberpunks have declared the subgenre past its expiration date, subtly distancing themselves at best and completely denouncing the movement at worst. Anderson takes issue with their exodus, writing, "like the original punks, we are beginning to call bullshit," adding, "We need their skepticism now, perhaps more than ever." Punk, cyberpunk, and hip-hop are all movements of malcontents replacing what they see with ever-new visions of how things should be. Cyberpunk achieved its revolution by re-envisioning science fiction.

### Atomic Punk

For our purposes, I will say that cyberpunk proper starts in 1982 and ends in 1999, from *Blade Runner* to *The Matrix*, from William Gibson's "Burning Chrome" to his *All Tomorrow's Parties*, from Grandmaster Flash and the Furious Five's "The Message" to Eminem letting everyone know his name, from our landing on "Planet Rock" to Mike Ladd welcoming us to the *Afterfuture*. There are works before and works since that embody the visions and values of cyberpunk, but these dates act as rough parameters for their assimilation into the larger social sphere, for the time it took cyberpunk to become cyberculture. In 1982 computers were more and more prevalent in the workplace but having one at home was still a big deal. By 1999 they were in every workplace and *not* having one at home was the big deal.

In his autobiography, computer scientist and author Rudy Rucker tells the story of catching the cyberpunk wave just as it was swelling toward the shore. Rucker already had two science fiction novels out, a third on the way, and was out to change the genre with a vengeance. He'd won the first Philip K. Dick Award in 1983 just after Dick died and met up with the reigning crop of the new movement. "I started hearing about a new writer called William Gibson," he writes. "I saw a copy of *Omni* with his story, 'Johnny Mnemonic'. I was awed by the writing. Gibson, too, was out to change SF. And we weren't the only ones." Around the same time, Bruce Sterling was publishing an SF zine called *Cheap Truth*. Rucker continues,

> Reading Bruce's sporadic mailings of *Cheap Truth*, I learned there were a number of other disgruntled and radicalized new SF writers like me. At first Bruce Sterling's zine didn't have any particular name for the emerging new SF movement — it wouldn't be until 1983 that the cyberpunk label would take hold.

It was in that year that Bruce Bethke inadvertently named the movement with the title of his short story "Cyberpunk." Gardner Dozois later used the term to describe the genre. Rucker told Clare Evans in 2012, "We started writing cyberpunk because we had a really strong discontent with the status quo in science fiction, and with the state of human society at large." In this revolution, the names Rucker, Gibson, and Sterling were loosely joined by John Shirley, Greg Bear, Pat Cadigan, and Lew Shiner. Cadigan sums it up, telling me,

> Cyberpunk was identified as such only after it had been around for a while. The original writers, myself included, didn't sit down and say, "Okay, what the world needs now is something called cyberpunk, and here it is." Cyberpunk was a reflection of the larger dissatisfaction and unrest in general, as well as a reaction against the old SF tropes.

In addition to those mentioned above, several other concerns and conventions mark cyberpunk in sharp contrast to its galaxy-hopping, alien-invaded precursors. Some of them include a globalized concept of the future with a nod to planet-spanning information networks and a more fluid mix of races and genders; technologies of information exchange and biological augmentation that contrast the fallibility of human "meat" against the structural integrity of silicon and metal (i.e., "meatspace" vs. "cyberspace"); the blurring boundaries between bodies and technologies, as well as internal and external memory and memories; post-industrial time-shifting technologies; subversions, extensions, and prostheses of trad sci-fi tropes; a juxtaposition of high-tech, corporate command-and-control systems (hence the "cyber") with the lo-fi, D.I.Y. underground (hence the "punk"); and antihero protagonists: involuntary rebels, down-on-their-luck loners, reluctant misfits, and outright outlaws.

While it sometimes seems a definitively 1980s affair, cyberpunk was often ardently so. It was post-punk and pre-web, yet wildly informed by punk-rock sensibilities, the onset of the personal computer, and the promise of the internet. These technologies sprouted through the cracks of our lives. They went from the far-flung possibilities of government institutions and academic think tanks to the most intimate interfaces of our days. We now use them to do laundry, to see better, to communicate with each other.

In the preface to Gibson's 1986 short-story collection, *Burning Chrome*, Sterling wrote that Gibson's early stories had made apparent "the hidden bulk of an iceberg of social change," an iceberg that the web's social warming has melted over the years since. In his later work, which is set in the present, Gibson writes in a world informed by his previous prophecies, a world David Punter describes as "cyber-Gothic." It is as if the present caught up with his projected future. The books, *Pattern Recognition* (2003), *Spook Country* (2007), and *Zero History* (2010), read like Gibson's earlier science fiction, yet their weird gadgets and odd characters are all present in our present. He's not making any of those things up. Anymore.

These aren't predictions of the future, they're a mythology of the near now.

## Parsing Patterns

Any web wanderer worth her bookmarks knows that William Gibson coined the term for the spaces and places that we all explore online. So strong was the word that one large software company attempted to trademark it for their own purposes. So many such ideas have been co-opted by others that Gibson has jokingly referred to himself as "the unpaid Bill." Our reliance on screens and networks is now taken for granted, but the idea wasn't evident until Gibson's work in the early 1980s. He saw an early ad for Apple Computers, and the idea hit him: "Everyone is going to have one of these, I thought, and everyone is going to want to live inside them. And somehow, I knew that the notional space behind all the computer screens would be one single universe." He saw the kids in video arcades playing coin-operated kiosks and could tell that they wanted to be inside the machines, playing together in a world other than ours. Gibson regularly responds to claims of his pre-cog abilities — the ones he used to predict and project the personal computer's connectivity and utter ubiquity — by saying that he's just exploring "an increasingly science fictional present."

Why does the world now look more like a William Gibson novel than one by Isaac Asimov or Arthur C. Clarke? Gibson's friend and cyberpunk peer Bruce Sterling says it's a matter of diet: "Clarke was spending all his time with Wernher von Braun, and Gibson was spending all his time listening to Velvet Underground albums and haunting junk stores in Vancouver." Gibson describes his early writing diet similarly:

When I started to write science fiction, I knew I was working in a genre that was traditionally deeply deprived of hipness. I went looking for ways to import as much rock-and-roll aesthetic into science fiction as was possible. Going back and listening to Steely Dan's lyrics, for instance, suggested a number of ways to do that. It seemed that there was a very hip, almost subversive science fiction aesthetic in Donald Fagen's lyrics which not many people have picked up on. But there's other stuff — David Bowie's *Diamond Dogs* album, which has this totally balls-out science fiction aesthetic going. The Velvet Underground, early Lou Reed — that was important. I thought, OK, that's the hip science fiction of our age, and so I'm going to try to write up to that standard, rather than trying to write up to Asimov.

In his debut novel, *Neuromancer* (1984), for instance, Gibson named the Linda Lee character after the Linda Lee in Velvet Underground's 1970 song "Cool It Down." Knowing the character in the song provides insight into the character in the book, like recognizing a sample in a rap song. These intertextual references will recur regularly as we proceed.

## *From Cyberpunk to Cyberculture*

Gibson's journey to this particular now hasn't been a direct path. He spent some time exploring other possible futures. Like Gibson, the rest of the Whole Earth Network migrated from the actual commune to the virtual community. Originally emerging from the counterculture of the late 1960s, they published their *Whole Earth Software Catalog* in 1985 and established their online bulletin board system, the Whole Earth 'Lectronic Link (the WELL), the following year. Their offbeat past informed our online present. "We don't quite live in the world that cyberpunk fiction predicted," says Bruce Bethke, "But we live in the world that the kids who grew up reading cyberpunk fiction built..." The Whole Earth hackers and cyber-hippies envisioned themselves as part of a giant, generational experiment. "Small-scale technologies would serve them in this work," Fred Turner writes, "Stereo gear, slide projectors, strobe lights, and, of course, LSD all had the power to transform the mind-set of an individual and to link him or her through invisible 'vibes' to others." Rucker quotes another hacker, writing, "Computers are to the eighties what LSD was to the sixties."

Gibson tuned in and dropped out as well, saying that reading Burroughs and the other Beats transformed him into Virginia's own "Patient Zero of what would later be called the counterculture." Mind-altering drugs were central to the movement but not essential to it. There was a sense that the straight world was ending, but the straight world and those counter to it collaborated on what was to come. Once Gibson and the other cyberpunks moved on to building the twenty-first century in their fiction, many of their like-minded, counterculture contemporaries were building it for real. Gibson told *Wired* in 1995, "I think bohemians are the subconscious of industrial society. Bohemians are like industrial society, dreaming." I like to think of hip-hop as a version of Gibson's bohemia, but I think it's a dreaming of a different kind. Mark Fisher wrote of the 2000s,

The story of this decade has been about the defeat of bohemia by business. Now business wants not only to control culture, but to be culture, too. On the other hand, culture prostrates itself before business, like a cowed kid sucking up to a swaggering bully.

Gibson cites punk as the last viable Bohemia. In 1996 Gibson claimed that the half-life of grunge — which, like punk, had by that time been subject to public and much-debated commercial co-opting — was about three weeks. Perhaps this says more about where Gibson's head was at the time than it does about the creativity of bohemian backwaters. After all, we've seen plenty of cool things happen in the intervening years, and Gibson was writing *Idoru*, one of his darker visions of modern culture, saturated with multi-channel, tabloid television, media surveillance, and deep datamining.

Sound familiar?

## *Ride the Fader*

Computer hackers represent the more hands-on application of the term "cyberpunk." Envisioned hunched over keyboards in dark basements, perusing information private, personal, political, financial, and otherwise, these shadowy figures are the enemy of all that is good about computer technology. They are cyberpunks made manifest in their darkest form.

In the broader view, hackers only steal if it's needed to create new worlds, new ways of doing things. Hackers are explorers, trespassers, provocateurs. They push their chosen technology to its limits. Hackers are creators, artists, activists. They take what's available and make it into more.

*The DJ cultivates and manages singularities: the bifurcation points on the edge of chaos, where dynamical systems manifest their emergent properties and transcend the sum of their elements. The speakers emit alchemical sounds, cut and pasted by needles in deep grooves, manipulated by human hands on black wax. It is a pastiche of ever-shifting, hand-engineered, sonic references. The dialectic of the two turntables unfolds in time. Beats juggled for the meat jungle. Scratches snatched for the daily catch. Crowd control, cruise control, remote control, the discotheque as panopticon: A command-control system with the DJ at the helm. Several systems work at odds and in conjunction to make waves in the scene. This is a language sans nouns; a lingua franca consisting only of verbs: motion, phase transition, aural morphology, all moving at the speed of left and right.*

*As the Universe of sound finds ears, vibrating shards meld into sonic calling cards: An ever-shifting musical identity that gives way to unrelenting multiplicity. Thanks to technology often perceived as obsolete, the entire history of sound is available for datamining. The DJ is an archeologist of vinyl plates. Digging in the crates, (s)he returns with pieces to the amorphous puzzle. A cartographer of soundscapes unknown and yet unformed, the DJ makes the map and the terrain simultaneously on the fly.*

Like the African Diaspora that invented it, hip-hop culture is made up of pieces previously spread all over the planet. Hip-hop music is a patchwork of the past. Its attendant culture borrows and builds from anything available. Yet one of the core tenets of hip-hop culture is "no biting," or plagiarizing. That is, one is not allowed to steal anyone else's style, lyrics, moves, and so on under any circumstances. The practice of sampling recorded pieces of music, vocals, and sounds is integral to the process by which hip-hop music is created. The pioneers of the genre used little more than records, turntables, and speakers. Manually manipulating moment-events, DJs hack the whole of recorded music, mining dusty crates of vinyl for just the right beats, breaks, and blasts. Bruce Sterling writes, "Scratch music, whose ghetto innovators turn the phonograph itself into an instrument, producing an archetypal Eighties music where funk meets Burroughs' cut-up method." These DJs are just continuing a tradition of previous misuses of technology by the Black diaspora such as broken bottlenecks on Blues guitar necks, oil drums as steel drums, and so on. Dery writes that "hip-hop culture retrofits, refunctions, and willfully misuses the technocommodities and science fictions generated by dominant culture." The many mannerisms of spinning and scratching DJs have a longer lineage than most imagine.

## A Saucerful of Secrets

Kool Herc had the sound system and Akfrika Bambaataa had the records, but Grandmaster Flash was hip-hop's first real hacker, its first cyberpunk. Driven to stand out in a quickly crowding DJ scene, the South Bronx native employed electronic engineering skills picked up at Samuel Gompers Vocational Technical High School to rig his turntable-mixer set-up. Flash explains:

> I couldn't afford a mixer with a built-in cue system where you could hear turntable one or two in advance. I had

to actually get a single pole-double throw switch, crazy glue it to the top of my mixer, build an external mix on the outside just strong enough to drive a headphone, so when you clicked it over you would hear the other turntable in advance. But this whole idea of hearing the cut ahead of time took three years to come into being.

He had seen other DJs lift and replace the needle on the record rather recklessly during their live sets. Building what he called a "peek-a-boo" system, his aim was to mix breaks and beats without having to do that. Hacking his mixer to let him hear and cue records before the party heard them, Flash could bend and blend songs and sounds as he saw fit. He also perfected backspins and scratches, allowing him make new compositions out of old compositions, live on the turntables. He worked tirelessly in his basement, forging and sharpening his new skills.

Quick Mixing: Grandmaster Flash. Photo by Mikael Väisänen.

When Flash debuted what he called his Quick Mix Theory, no one could quite follow him. "I had come up with all my new methods and techniques and I had perfected them," Flash writes, excited at the possibilities he'd uncovered. "I was sure everybody who heard my new style would feel the same thing. I was wrong." Flash's debut in the park was a disaster. He seamlessly mixed and chopped and extended, rearranging the structure of song after song. "*And nobody got it!*" One promoter later called it "turntable acrobatics," adding, "I was just watching him and thinking, 'God what is he doing?!' I was just awe-struck." Fab 5 Freddy described Flash's techniques as being "from another planet." Flash emerged from his basement ahead of the rest of the world. Everyone else had to catch up.

Though Dr. Dre cites seeing Clinton's Parliament-Funkadelic in concert in LA as the event that opened his mind to music without limits, he also says, "My first exposure to hip-hop was 'The Adventures of Grandmaster Flash on the Wheels of Steel'. That's what started me deejaying. I think I was about 15." Released in 1981, Flash's "Adventures..." remains the ultimate DJ cut, a cut-and-pasted collage of bits, beats, basslines, and spoken vocal samples from Chic, Queen, Blondie, Michael Viner's Incredible Bongo Band, the Hellers, Sugarhill Gang, Sequence and Spoonie Gee, and his own Furious Five. This record and Afrika Bambaataa and the Soulsonic Force's "Planet Rock," which combines everything from Kraftwerk to Sergio Leone, provide the cornerstone of hip-hop composition. "To understand the magnificent creativity of the hip-hop DJ and the logical progression of today's masters is to listen closely to both these cuts," writes CK Smart.

## Boogie Down Predictions

"Hip-hop humanizes technology and makes it tactile," says Harry Allen. "In hip-hop, you make the technology do stuff that it isn't supposed to do, get music out of something that's not supposed to give you music quite that way. You squeeze it, rip at it, and do other things with the equipment that mess viciously with your warranty." Voiding warranties is a byproduct of core hacker activities. Hackers believe that access to knowledge should be unhindered, access to tools should be total.

Kool Herc started the end-of-the-world B-boy party, Bambaataa brought the alien sounds, but Grandmaster Flash hacked the technology and created a science. Sampling technology eventually caught up with the DJs and made the practice of reanimating the past a staple of music production. The cultural practice went far beyond just sounds though. "From my perspective," André Sirois a.k.a. DJ Food Stamp writes in his book *Hip-Hop DJs and the Evolution of Technology*, "what these South Bronx DJs started was the foundation of the new media ideology present in popular culture today: sample, mix, burn, share, and repeat." Sirois argues that in its complexity, hip-hop culture is itself a new media culture. Current so-called "new media" can be traced back from smartphones and the internet to landlines and the telegraph. Following DJs' hacking of recording technology and playback from Flash's mixer toggle-switch and Grand Wizard Theodore's manual scratch to digital sampling and DJ software, Sirois historicizes the technical evolution and cultural practices of hip-hop DJs as new media. Emphasizing the network mentality present from the beginning of hip-hop, he employs an open-source metaphor to characterize the culture.

Through the free exchange of ideas and the cooperation of numerous hackers, the open source software movement has given us the Linux operating system and free software of all sorts, as well as many aspects of the internet. While hip-hop is largely a battle-borne culture, the competition has always been tempered by cooperation and collaboration. Where DJs, emcees, B-boys, or graffiti writers compete for dominance and bragging rights, they also share techniques, tools, and work together in crews and teams. Competition fuels creativity, but collaboration fosters and forges it. Writing on innovation, authorship, and intellectual property, Sirois warns against romanticizing this collaboration. "From what I have seen," he writes, "when culture and industry converge, money and credit are given to some and not others, which compromises individual legacies, and then 'viruses' enter the network and undermine the open source logic that is at the heart of the culture." The industry operates from the top down, manipulating the DJs' "subcultural capital" as brands and intellectual properties. To that end, Sirois also covers how DJs perform sometimes unpaid and unrecognized research and development, from Flash's self-styled innovations to signature models of more modern turntablists, through the "dialectic between hip-hop DJs and the DJ product industry." His examples offer interesting case studies of bottom-up innovation but also illustrate how branding operates in the larger culture.

Sirois's concerns echo those of Gibson above regarding the co-opting of subcultures. Hip-hop is bohemian in Gibson's sense, but it's a different kind. Like the Gothic and the punk that precede it, hip-hop distorts the dominant culture, making it into something new. Its being borne of technology and built out of older music obscures its co-opting. A line between art and commerce that we erroneously consider stable in other genres is severed asunder by sampling. While hacking older media to make new media has always been around, it's never been quite like this.

Welcome to Planet Rock: Afrika Bambaataa.
Collage by Paul Insect.

## Chapter Three

# FRUIT OF THE LOOT

"This confusion and breaking of codes, this disrespect for previous authorities, boundaries, and rules, also exposes what was previously subordinate and hidden. Different histories become available, their languages drawn into contemporary eclecticism — producing unexpected encounters in the record grooves, on the dancefloor, and in everyday life."
— Iain Chambers, *Popular Culture: The Metropolitan Experience*

"For a fragment of the past to be touched by the present, there must be no continuity between them."
— Walter Benjamin, *The Arcades Project*

"The White man will never admit his real references. He will steal everything you have and still call you those names. He will drag out standards and talk about propriety."
— PaPa LaBas, in Ishmael Reed's *Mumbo Jumbo*

At the end of the 1980s, it was finally evident that something needed to be done about computer hacking. The online gangs and gangsters were either shut down, locked up, or on the run. White kids, would-be white-collar criminals, with mafia names and big, big talk and text behind keyboards and screens were scattering under federal scrutiny. The Legion of Doom disbanded, the Masters of Deception were shut down, Kevin Mitnick was in jail. In January of 1990, as if to start off the new decade in charge, the Secret Service raided the bedrooms of M.O.D. members Phiber Optik, Acid Phreak, and Scorpion. Their computers, notebooks, files, and floppies were all confiscated.

As the surveillance of their activity has expanded from phone logs to wireless taps, hackers have evolved from phone phreaking to secret leaking. It's a ratcheting up of tactics and attacks on both sides. Aaron Swartz, Chelsea Manning, Adrian Lamo, Aaron Barr, and Edward Snowden have all been pawns and prisoners of this information warfare. Bruce Sterling's 1992 book *The Hacker Crackdown* which, after chronicling the early history of computer hacker activity, investigation, and incarceration, states ominously, "It is the End of the Amateurs."

These quips and quotes can be applied to either side.

The Hacker Ethic states that access to computers "and anything which might teach you something about the way the world works should be unlimited and total." Hackers of this kind seek to understand, not to undermine. And they tolerate no constraints. Tactical media, so-called to avoid the semiotic baggage of related labels, exploits the asymmetry of knowledge gained via hacking. Hackers use these everyday tactics to pry open new spaces of resistance and discourse. As we will see, the circulation of ideas via invisible, informal networks and the hijacking of media messages are two ways hackers resist. In her book *Tactical*

*Media*, Rita Raley writes, "*See what I have made*, the tactical user says. *See how I try to manage the ties that bind and produce me.*" It's a tale of rogues gone straight, straights gone rogue, and the weird gone pro. It's a battle over stiffly defined contexts, lines drawn and defended. Informal groups of information insurgents like the crews behind Wikileaks and Anonymous keep open tabs on the powers that would be.

Hackers are easy to defend when they're on your side. Wires may be wormholes, but that can be dangerous when they flow both ways. Once you get locked out of all your accounts and the contents of your hard drive end up on the wrong screen, the hackers aren't your friends anymore. When hackers take your information or your hard work for their own purposes, something must break.

### Fear of a Hacked Planet

At the end of the 1980s, it was finally evident that something needed to be done about digital sampling. Hip-hop producers were making money off of the talent and toil of other artists. This would not stand! The Turtles sued De La Soul for $1.7 million, Gilbert O'Sullivan went after Biz Markie, the Beastie Boys spent a quarter of a million dollars clearing samples for their cluttered kaleidoscope, 1989's *Paul's Boutique*. In another case of technology and culture outpacing The Law, the sampling crackdown coincided with the hacker crackdown.

One of the most recognizable cultural contributions of rap music is sampling. In its simplest form, a sample is a piece of previously recorded sound, mechanically lifted from its original context, and arranged into a new composition. In hip-hop, samples were originally manipulated using turntables and vinyl records, but the practice has since largely moved on to more efficient digital samplers. Commerce and copyright laws notwithstanding, anything that has been recorded can be used as a sample (e.g., beats, guitar riffs, bass lines, vocals, horn blasts, etc.). "Using everything from drum pads and samplers to magpie the last few centuries of speeches, music, and commercials and turn them upside-in for the betterment of the practitioner and listener," emcee and producer Juice Aleem tells me. "Hip-hop is hacking." Sampling technology allows producers to make new compositions out of old ones, using old outputs as new inputs, like a hacker cobbling together code for a new program or purpose.

The first example of this sort of sound hacking on the Billboard charts was a 1956 song called "The Flying Saucer" by Bill Buchanan and Dickie Goodman. The two collaged clips of songs of the time together on a reel-to-reel magnetic tape recorder creating a ridiculous alien-invasion scenario. Four record labels sued the two composers and lost. The judge deemed their looting a new and original work.

Mining the past for samples and sounds, hip-hop hacks recorded sound for self-expression, and, like cyberpunk, hip-hop has spread around the world. Both are a part of a globalized network culture that decentralizes the human subject's stability in space and time and in which the technologically mediated subject reforms and remixes ideas of body normativity. With everything from clothes and glasses to tattoos and piercings, technology changes what is considered normal to have on or in your body.

Cybernetics, the science of command-control systems and from hence the "cyber" in "cyberpunk," defines humans as "information-processing systems whose boundaries are determined by the flow of information." Technologically reproduced memories disrupt more than just body normativity: media theorist Marshall McLuhan once declared that an individual is a "montage of loosely assembled parts," and furthermore that when you are on the phone, you don't have a body. Technology dismembers the body. Our media might be "extensions of ourselves" in McLuhan's terms, but they're also prosthetics, amputating parts as they extend them.

Public Enemy: Chuck D. Collage by Ian Wright.

Grandmaster Flash once described another DJ as using "his hands like a heart surgeon." In his book on Public Enemy's undisputed and sample-heavy classic, 1988's *It Takes a Nation of Millions to Hold Us Back*, Christopher R. Weingarten draws a lengthy and effective analogy between records and the body, casting samples as organ transplants. Tales of transplanted organs causing their recipients to adopt the tastes and behaviors of their dead donors read like the "meatspace" anxieties of cyberpunk:

> A 68-year-old woman suddenly craves the favorite foods of her 18-year-old heart donor, a 56-year-old professor gets strange flashes of light in his dreams and learns that his donor was a cop who was shot in the face by a drug dealer. Does a sample on a record work the same way? Can the essence of a hip-hop record be found in the motives, emotions and energies of the artists it samples? Is it likely that something an artist intended 20 years ago will re-emerge anew?

Conceived as a combination of the hip-hop of Run-DMC and the punk rock of the Clash, Public Enemy emerged from Strong Island, New York in the late 1980s. Made up of emcees Chuck D and Flavor Flav, DJ Terminator X, and Professor Griff and the S1Ws (the Security of the First World), their paramilitary dance squad, P.E. upended not only what hip-hop could be but the power of sound itself. Their production team, the Bomb Squad (Eric "Vietnam" Sadler, brothers Hank and Keith Shocklee, as well as Chuck D) used upwards of forty-eight separate recording tracks to build their apocalyptic collages. Where their 1987 debut,

*Yo! Bumrush the Show* relied on live instrumentation in addition to sampling, *Nation of Millions* is one of the most sample-ridden recordings ever made, its layers coalescing and collapsing, its chaos barely contained. Scott Herren says of the record, "it sounded like science fiction." It remains one of the boldest sonic statements not only in hip-hop but in all of modern music. The Bomb Squad experimented in the studio like Dr. Frankenstein in his laboratory. They built a body out of noise, and it came alive, thrashing everything in its past and in its path, including copyright law.

Public Enemy: *It Takes a Nation of Millions to Hold Us Back.*

Though Russell Simmons called them "Black punk rock," Public Enemy stated: "We're media hijackers." About the song "Caught, Can We Get a Witness" from *Nation of Millions*, Chuck D says, "We got sued religiously after the fact, but not at that time. The song itself was just challenging the purpose of it":

> *Found this mineral that I call a beat*
> *Paid zero*
> *I packed my load 'cause it's better than gold*
> *People don't ask the price, but it's sold*

Chuck's use of the word "witness" is curious in our current context. "Cultural memory is most forcefully transmitted through the individual voice and body," Hirsch and Smith write, "through the testimony of a witness." In occult practices, a *witness* is an object that can link people across times, just as musical samples do. To establish such a connection is called a *witness effect*. Preston Nichols explains, "As a noun, it refers to an object that is connected or related to someone or something [...] As a verb, 'witness' means to use an object to enter a person's consciousness or otherwise have an effect on them." A lock of hair, a piece of clothing, a proper beat, bassline, or vocal sample — any of these could have that bridging effect, tying two separate times together. The song ends: "They say that I stole this. I rebel with a raised fist; can we get a witness?" When their future is outlawed, the outlaws become the future.

## *Atemporal Minded*

Two forces, futures yet seen and the past reproduced, lift hip-hop out of time. It exists in a floating atemporality. It's an example of what Kodwo Eshun describes as a reversal of the avant-garde revolt "against a power structure that relied on control and representation of the historical archive." He continues, "Afrofuturism approaches contemporary music as an intertext of recurring literary quotations that may be cited and used as statements capable of imaginatively reordering chronology and fantasizing history." An intertextual view of texts emphasizes their historicity. In *The Man in the High Castle*, Philip K. Dick defines "historicity" as "when a thing has history in it." The many allusions woven together through samples and rhymes give hip-hop a historicity that many other musical genres maintain in sound but not as much in their lyrics. Though a dialog between social reality and its fictional futures has occurred since we started telling stories, mechanical reproduction has made the exchange easier, more widespread, and more difficult to parse. German critical theorist Walter Benjamin anticipated at least a few of the digital dilemmas we face in the twenty-first century in his landmark 1935 essay, "The Work of Art in the Age of Mechanical Reproduction." Of all forms of art, music seemed to be the least of Benjamin's concerns, but I find it difficult to even read the name of his most famous writing without immediately thinking of hip-hop DJs. One seems to evoke the other so directly that such an analysis seems obvious. According to Benjamin, the recording of music makes it into a commodity and gives it its exchange value. Once recordings become fetishized by collectors, the artifacts accrue their cultic value. The basic argument of Benjamin's essay stems from this shift in value. He writes that an original piece of artwork possesses an aura, a halo of authenticity. Mechanical reproduction, though it democratizes the experience of art, releases this aura. Eshun adds,

> I think one important idea that emerges when one looks back on that moment of the mid-to-late 1980s is that artists became concerned with questions of memory, that they became discontented with, to put it crudely, the normative languages around history, heritage, nationality, and memorialization. The questions of memory and duration then emerged as key sites of aesthetic engagement.

## Raiding the Archives

The selection of particular information to be saved or archived is an act that predisposes that information for attention in the future. What we record receives future attention just by dint of being recorded. We think of archives as collections of things in the past tense, but we use them to save those things for future use. The past matters here not because of historical events as they were recorded, but because of the possibilities of those that were not. Recording is a form of writing. McLuhan went so far as to state that, "the brief and compressed history of the phonograph includes all phases of the written, the printed, and the mechanized word." The turntable is a mechanism for rewriting recorded histories. Grandmaster DXT, best known as the DJ who did the scratches on Herbie Hancock's hit song from 1983, "Rockit," even refers to Grandmaster Flash's original DJ innovations as "editing." Writing, rewriting, editing, citing, reciting, mixing, remixing — all of these practices involve sampling in some form. We use the past to build futures not yet forgotten. Not only are we afraid to forget, but we want our histories at hand because we fear the future as well.

Unlike the oral testimony, the archive has no addressee. To quote from records removes their original context, which Benjamin contended led to a loss of meaning. When the archives move from written, printed, and other physical documents to digital databases, meanings and contexts hang together more loosely and drift more easily.

Seemingly attempting to hold these slippery pieces in place, copyright law loses its grip the further these quotations spread form their original sources. For instance, the 1987 song "It's Tricky" by Run-DMC is primarily constructed from two previous songs. The musical track samples the guitars from "My Sharona" by the Knack, and the hook is an interpolation of the chorus from the 1981 cheerleading hit "Mickey" by Toni Basil. Explaining the old-school origins of the song, DMC says, "I just changed the chorus around and talked about how this rap business can be tricky to a brother." Tricky indeed: twenty years after the song was released, Berton Averre and Doug Fieger of the Knack sued Run-DMC for unauthorized use of their song. "That sound is not only the essence of 'My Sharona', it is one of the most recognizable sounds in rock 'n' roll," says Fieger, the Knack's lead singer. As true as that is, it's not the most recognizable element of Run-DMC's hit. That honor belongs to Basil's "Mickey."

Like "Grandmaster Flash's Adventures on the Wheels of Steel," one of hip-hop's earliest deliberate glimpses of the future — in several additional ways — was "Planet Rock" by Afrika Bambaataa and the Soulsonic Force. Lyrically the song imagined an alternate world, on which everyone celebrated harmony and humanity. The song is mostly known for its unique sound though. Produced by Arthur Baker, the song lifted samples from computer-heavy Krautrock band Kraftwerk. Baker had spotted B-boys getting down to the Germans' robotic electro-funk and envisioned the next step: he added the block-rocking beats of his new Roland TR-808 drum machine and a new era was born. As writer Nelson George describes it, "The sound of 'Planet Rock' is like a spaceship landing in the ghetto."

Not everyone was so enthusiastic about seeing the new era envisioned on "Planet Rock" though. Wolfgang Flür, once a member of Kraftwerk, writes about Baker and Bambaataa in his autobiography,

The pair put together a hip-hop rap album on which they mixed parts of "Numbers" and "Trans-Europe Express" for a single release, turning out an American-style piece of music. They didn't even ask in the first place whether Kraftwerk was in agreement with this, let alone pay for the use of the samples. This is the nastiest kind of theft!

In another example, a two-second, drum loop from Kraftwerk's 1977 song "Metal on Metal" was the backbone of the 1997 single "Nur mir" by Sabrina Setlur. Kraftwerk's Ralf Hütter sued producer Moses Pelham over the unauthorized use of the clip, only to finally lose the case in 2016. Though not involved in the suit, Flür continues, "[...] such uses of other artists' musical property for these kinds of purposes are often tasteless and tend to damage the original."

Whether violating copyrights or legitimately quoting archived sounds, hip-hop producers must continually add on with their contributions while maintaining the culture's heritage. That is, a producer or practitioner must make something new while still adhering to the rules of hip-hop. Philosopher of science Thomas Kuhn, the guy who gave us the idea of paradigm shifts, once posited an essential tension in science between innovation and tradition: too innovative and the theory is untestable, too traditional and it's not useful. The same tension can be said to exist in hip-hop, as if one "innovates" without regard to "tradition," one is no longer doing hip-hop. Where samples and loops are concerned, one must not adhere too closely to the original source lest one be accused of rote repetition at best and plagiarism or biting at worst. "What separates 'biting' and 'enlightening' is the difference between *repetition* and repetition *with a difference*," Adam Bradley writes. It's a delicate balance to be sure, and one of which a violation is sometimes difficult to discern.

Many still see sampling as cut-and-paste coattail-riding. Flür continues, "To my ears, the whole orgy of remixing and releasing cover versions that has spread like a plague throughout the entire music industry since 1982 is mostly detrimental rubbish." Though he's an avid user of samplers himself, RZA of the Wu-Tang Clan understands Flür's viewpoint. "A lot of people still don't recognize the sampler as a musical instrument," RZA writes. "I can see why. A lot of rap hits over the years used the sampler more like a Xerox machine." Of RZA's own sampling techniques, Greg Tate writes,

> If Public Enemy brought microsurgery to hip-hop collage, RZA brings a sculptural hand closer to the source than Cubism. Like an African carver, his Orientalist exaggerations of old-school soul songs forms sounds organic rather than grafted. In this respect Tricky and RZA are similar: they both use samplers in a way that suggests they're working with flesh rather than found objects.

Tate defends sampling as an artistic practice, calling it not a copycat act but a folk form of reanimation. "Hip-hop is ancestor worship," he writes. In its Kraftwerk ruling, the German Constitutional Court agrees, acknowledging sampling as one of hip-hop's "style-defining elements," adding that blocking "Nur mir" would "practically exclude the creation of pieces of music in a particular style." The irony of the copyright laws, their enforcement, and the boutique sample-clearing industry that emerged in the late 1980s is that they kill creativity by making it easier to sample and loop one song than to collage a bunch of songs into something utterly unique. By 1991 the multilayered sonic tapestries of Public Enemy's *It Takes a Nation of Millions…*, De La Soul's *3 Feet High and Rising*, and the Beastie Boys' *Paul's Boutique* were prohibitively expensive because every sample and snippet meant more artists to be paid. Looping the elements of one song, which operates much like doing a cover version, was still financially viable because there was only one person to pay. It's the difference between paying for something hand-built piece by piece and paying for it prefabricated all at once. It's the difference between creating something new and curating something old.

The sampling of previously recorded slices of sound, at first by repeating them live with two copies of the same record on two turntables, is a case of mechanical reproduction catching up with the cultural practices of hip-hop, of technology catching up with what human minds and hands were already doing. With the spread of mechanical reproduction, as well as sampling and referencing as cultural practices, throughout media and technological artifacts, mediated memories are now mass produced, reproduced, and shared. To most of us though, the sharing of mediated memories, of cultural allusions, bonds us and gives us a sense of belonging. A lot of this togetherness is due to the technological reproduction of media. The media of the twenty-first century is rife with references to previous media in a manner unseen in previous eras. Samples, allusions, adaptations, remakes, remixes, and copies are now all norms of media and art.

### Memories Don't Live Like People Do

"Cinematographic and phonographic recordings can repeat themselves accurately and indefinitely," writes Domietta Torlasco, "bringing about the recurrence of the past of which they are the indexical trace." The *indexical trace* is a semiotic concept in which an object has no resemblance to the object signified yet points to the signified using a sensory element. Introduced by Paul Kane in 2007, an indexical trace might be the smell of a soup, the sound of the footsteps of a person, or a flag showing the waves of the wind — a ghost of the thing. A sample appropriated and manipulated, a lyric interpolated, a paraphrase or parody — these are all indexical traces owing their form to the originals but not quite resembling them. Recordings of all kinds are indexical traces of the performances they capture. Sampling pushes them even further afield, creating phantom traces of events that never occurred and never could. These traces point as much to the past as they do to possible futures: retrievals without resemblance.

In Ridley Scott's classic cyberpunk movie *Blade Runner*, the advanced humanoid androids, known as Replicants, base their "human" pasts on implanted memories. Their intelligence, though impressive, is not grounded in a larger cognitive context. They are programmed with memories to make them more human, imbued with the personal archives of another. They adopt "alienated experiences and narratives which they take to be their own, and which they subsequently make their own through use." As Tyrell Corporation's CEO Dr. Eldon Tyrell, creator of the Replicants, explains to Rick Deckard,

> We began to recognize in them a strange obsession. After all they are emotionally inexperienced with only a few years in which to store up the experiences which you and I take for granted. If we gift them a past, we create a cushion or pillow for their emotions and consequently we can control them better.

Like the stories we share through various means, these implanted, mediated, or "prosthetic memories," don't come from our lived experience. This represents a crisis of authenticity for Benjamin, something that is "simply lived through rather than meaningfully experienced." In the face of our day-to-day complications — much like the Replicants in *Blade Runner* — we long for times we never knew. Some argue that this makes us victims of the corporate commodification of culture, suggesting that we're no better than Replicants, walking around with prosthetic memories courtesy of the mass media and its rampant reproduction of artifacts. As Benjamin writes,

> [...] technical reproduction can put the copy of the original into situations which would be out of reach for the original itself. Above all, it enables the original to meet the beholder halfway, be it in the form of a photograph or a phonograph record.

When Deckard explains to the Replicant Rachael that her memories are not her own, that the photograph she has of herself as a little girl is not her, he authenticates not her past but her present. Although false, the photograph is her document of her history. History "is only constituted if we look at it, excluded from it." That is, "history" is the process of historical causality and also the narrative retelling of that causality. And nostalgia only works if the original has been forgotten, or in this case, never existed for the subject in the first place.

For another example, in Charles Yu's 2010 novel, *How to Live Safely in a Science Fictional Universe*, the narrator, a time-machine mechanic, defines nostalgia as a, "Weak but detectable interaction between two neighboring universes that are otherwise not causally connected." The Celtics call them "thin spaces," places where the boundary between our world and the next are noticeably thinner. In thin places, we are able to realize our more essential selves. According to Yu, nostalgia "Manifests itself in humans as a feeling of missing a place one has never been, a place very much like one's home universe, or as a longing for versions of one's self that one will never, and can never know."

Replicants are obsessed with photographs. Where the Replicants can't be sure of what they know, the pictures provide a visual totem, a physical connection to the implanted "cushion" of their memories. Where such photographs, as well as phonograph records, are reproductions of scenes and sounds respectively, those forms have given way to digital reproductions of both. The remediation of these elements represents a crisis of context when we use filters on digital photos to make them look old and digital effects on recordings to make them sound like scratchy vinyl. It's not only longing but also the undermining of that longing. Memory and identity are inextricably bound together. Nostalgia is another indication that where you're from and where you're at are at odds with each other.

If we cannot locate where our memories originate, our very humanity is at stake. Many have argued that our lived experience has been increasingly slipping into technological mediation and representation. Based on this idea and the rampant branding and advertising covering any surface, Kalle Lasn argues that our culture has inducted

Replicant Memories: *Blade Runner*.

us into a cult: "By consensus, cult members speak a kind of corporate Esperanto: words and ideas sucked up from TV and advertising." Indeed, we quote television shows, allude to fictional characters and situations, and repeat song lyrics and slogans in everyday conversations. Lasn argues that we didn't choose these roles or behavior. Young people growing up in this environment risk their reality. As Simon Reynolds writes, "[Pop] is still considered the domain of the young, and young people aren't supposed to be nostalgic; they haven't been around long enough to build up a backlog of precious memories." But... *If we gift them a past, we can control them better.*

Benjamin was certainly concerned with the question of whether mass culture is a site of exploitation or emancipation, however he was equally concerned with authenticity. "The presence of the original is the prerequisite to the concept of authenticity," he writes. The empty nostalgia of our implanted memories holds no original and no original context.

One of the most distinctive features of noir-Gothic, cyberpunk works like *Blade Runner* is their residual past. Like recognizable samples in hip-hop tracks, extant structures poke through the rain and darkness of a once-future Los Angeles. Union Station, the Bradbury Building, and Frank Lloyd Wright's Ennis Brown house intermingle with sky-scorching smokestacks, video-billboard blimps, and the pyramid-like headquarters of the Tyrell Corporation. Norman M. Klein writes that the first four minutes of the film "represent layers of nostalgia, each built by a different technology from a different era." Those familiar structures are uncanny, like hearing a cover song and knowing the words but not quite recognizing the source. The filmmakers looted leftovers from other movies, household items, and children's toys to build those sets. There's a Millennium Falcon model, an upturned sink, and pieces from other parts of *Blade Runner* stacked in the background. The skyline stands as the indexical trace of a horizon never to come.

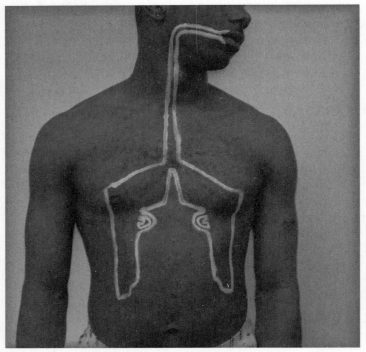
Nature of the Threat: Ras Kass. Photo by B+.

## Chapter Four

# SPOKEN WINDOWS

"I'll master your language, and in the meantime, I'll create my own."
— Tricky, "Christiansands"

"Language itself is a gamble. A roll of dice. The way you formulate your sentence, the words you pick and make that sentence, is the roll of the dice. That's why I'm a rapper, I pick the best words for the sentence. If your gamble rolls right, you'll win."
— Rammellzee, *RAMM-ELL-ZEE*

"It is not that I have no past. Rather, it continually fragments on the terrible and vivid ephemera of now."
— The Kid, in Samuel R. Delany's *Dhalgren*

William Melvin Kelley's debut novel, *A Different Drummer*, imagines another America, one where a slave revolt reconfigured the outcome of the Civil War and the nation thereafter. Three weeks before its release in 1962, Kelley twisted the term "woke" into its current parlance in a *New York Times* op-ed piece. His central point was that the African Diaspora was responsible for the cool, "beatnik" slang of the day (e.g., "chick," "dig," and "cool" itself, among others).

Though some of it stays in predominantly hip-hop contexts, the same can be claimed for hip-hop slang now. Quite a lot of it has traveled the wider world.

Each of our artifacts is "a kind of word, a metaphor that translates experience from one form to another." McLuhan pointed out that advertising employs the same strategies as poetry. If we treat archives and records, as well as software and cities, as artifacts, the emergent form seems to be the evolution of language itself: causal, casual language. New slang circulates from urban areas to music and online services.

One recent study maps the conflation of urban populations, new media, and the evolution of language. The researchers collected tweets containing new words and built a mathematical model that shows the flow of those words between cities. Just as Kelley claimed above, those areas with large African-American populations tend to be the leaders of such linguistic innovation. Slang that would normally remain isolated in one urban area until picked up by some mass medium or transmitted by traveling users is now narrowcast via networks. Innovators of utterances share their new words without ever seeing each other's cities.

The widespread dissemination of words and language is nothing new. Poetry and songs moved via spoken word, the printing press enabled broadsheets, Bibles, and other books to circulate. Even where literature outpaced literacy, books were often read aloud. Though Gutenberg's printing press is what made large-volume printed information a personal, portable phenomenon, the advent of the telegraph brought forth the initial singularity in the evolution of information technology. The telegraph separated communication from transportation. As news on the wire, information could thereafter spread and travel free from human hands. Information was thereby commoditized. Liberated from books and newspapers, new slang and ideas have since become a larger part of our culture.

The telegraph is so far antiquated in the landscape of communication technology, simply bringing it up in a serious manner seems almost silly. It's not unlike using a word that has been displaced by new ones. Words are metaphors, and metaphors are expressions of the unknown in terms of the known. Once a new word is known, it becomes assimilated into the larger language system. McLuhan once wrote that language in an electronic context would return us to "the Africa within." Slang expressions are passwords, keywords, shibboleths, codes.

### Head Space

As much as we think of our media as outside of our selves, we carry a great deal of that cargo around in our heads: the movies we've watched, the things we've read, the songs we've heard, and indeed, the lyrics we've learned. Think about the difference between reading an obscure, out-of-print book versus a recent bestseller. With the former, you're not likely to share the experience with many others and finding those others might be rather difficult. With the latter, you can join book clubs, online forums, and other discussions with the thousands of others who've read the same text. You can share your experience with them. The same overlapping of experience happens with movies, music, and other shared media. A "socio-textual community" like hip-hop is largely constituted by shared memories in the minds of members of that community.

One of my favorite hip-hop studio stories is from the recording of the duet between Jay-Z and the Notorious B.I.G., "Brooklyn's Finest" from Jay-Z's 1996 debut, *Reasonable Doubt*. Jay-Z and Biggie were sitting in the legendary D&D Studios in New York City listening to a beat by Clark Kent, a pen and a pad on the table between them. "They're both looking at the pad like, Go ahead, you take it. No, you take it," says Roc-A-Fella Records co-founder Biggs, "That's when they found out that both of them don't write." That is, neither of these emcees write any of their rhymes down. They write, edit, and recite straight out of their heads.

The Middle Passage of chattel slavery was one where the culture that survived was the one that could be carried in one's head. The ancient traditions of the motherland had to be remembered because the artifacts — buildings, sculptures, paintings, and so on — couldn't be carried. As much as it does with samples and remixing, hip-hop uses language to manipulate the larger culture. In this mediated battle for attention and memory, emcees trick our brains to remember. We carry their coded language in our heads.

The so-named "Hip-Hop Nation" is a textual community constituted by communicative action, discursive practices, and shared memories. The figurative language we find in hip-hop lyrics is inherent in African-American culture. Trickster tales, Toasts, chants, and so on predate and inform its texts today. Rap's lineage is linked with an oral culture that itself stretches across oceans, lands, ages, and generations. "So many people can't see that every great rapper is not just a documentarian, but a trickster," writes Jay-Z, "that every great rapper has a little bit of Chuck and a little bit of Flav in them..." The signifyin' practice of sampling and manipulating sounds carries over into the lyrical aspect in the form of allusions to previous songs and other media. The underlying idea is still to take what's there and make it your own, to release the Africa within. These scripts were made for flipping.

In his book *Decoded*, Jay-Z channels McLuhan and one of his most confounding theories in his explication here:

> When I was a kid the debate was LL versus Run-DMC, or, later, Kane versus Rakim. Next year it might be Drake versus J. Cole. It's a tribute to how deeply felt hip-hop is that people don't just sit back and listen to the music — they have to break it down, pick the lyrics apart, and debate the shit with other fans who are doing the same thing. When people talk about forms of media, sometimes they compare lean-forward media (which are interactive, like video games or the internet) and lean-back media (which are passive, like television or magazines). Music can be lean-back sort of media, it can just wash over you or play in the background — but hip-hop is different. It forces people to lean forward — lean right out of their chairs — and take a position.

A "lean-forward" medium in Jay-Z's terms is what McLuhan would call "cool," and a "lean-back" medium would be "hot": "any hot medium allows less participation than a cool one, as a lecture makes for less participation than a seminar, and a book for less than dialogue." With this bit of armchair media theory, Jay-Z is attributing to his genre more engagement with the audience than other genres of music. He's giving hip-hop — and in the process, himself — more power by making this comparison to other media. The power might be merely symbolic, but in the empire of signs, symbolic power is significant. Jay-Z explains further,

> After Barack was elected, I realized that the same thing hip-hop had been doing for years with language and brands — that is, reinventing them to mean something different from what they originally meant — we could now do to American icons like the flag. Things that had once symbolized slavery, oppression, militarism, and hypocrisy might now begin to legitimately represent us. We're not there yet, but Barack's election offered a tantalizing hint of what that might look like, including things like having the American "first lady" be a beautiful black woman who could trace her ancestry to American slaves.

Here he addresses the entire history of Black America, from slavery to the presidency. Like hip-hop's textual community, it is a discourse of transformation, of taking what one is given and making it into something new. Code is not poetry, but poetry can recode. Emcees' creative use of figurative language and wordplay are like employing cheat codes to access our memories. Along with slang, metaphor, simile, assonance, alliteration, and other literary forms, there are several other techniques specific to rap lyricists. Rhyme, rhythm, and allusion provide a versatile set of tools for the adept emcee.

## Rhyme Pays

The normal flow of time is often disrupted by the recurrence of something familiar in an unfamiliar context. Coincidences and synchronicities, memories jarred out of time by something in our present. We give a heightened sense of meaning in the presence of patterns perceived in events or words beyond their normal references and resonances. The poetic functions of language employ these patterns to imply connections with deeper meanings and structures. Rhyme is just such a pattern not present in other forms of writing.

Perhaps the most definitive aspect of rap is the rhyme, but it's also perhaps its most effective mnemonic device. Lyrics, phrases, and aphorisms that rhyme are easier to remember. We are also more likely to believe them. One simple study illustrated this phenomenon. Researchers had subjects compare rhyming and nonrhyming aphorisms. Consider the following:

*Birds of a feather flock conjointly.*
*Woes unite enemies.*
*Life is mostly struggle.*

As much as you might find truth in these statements or agree with their sentiments, remembering them could present a challenge. Compare them to the following:

*Birds of a feather flock together.*
*Woes unite foes.*
*Life is mostly strife.*

The difference is striking. Though we're not likely to admit it openly, we are more comfortable believing the latter set of constructions even though their truths remain unchanged.

Some argue that these results are unsurprising because there is an underlying poetry to the way we see the world. That is, our understanding of reality is fundamentally poetic, so poetic language naturally resonates with our sense of reason. Others argue that poetry conjures magic. All of these arguments are easy for a rap fan to agree with, and there are innumerable examples to cite. After all, rhyming is what rappers do. Let's look at a few less obvious kinds of rhyme.

Another example of the magic of combining rhyme and meaning in a dynamic way is the use of homonyms. Homonyms are words that are spelled the same or sound the same but have different meanings. They seem to be the same word, and thankfully they're not often used in close proximity in normal speech. If used with skill though, they can be quite effective. Here's an example from Kanye West's song "Heard 'Em Say":

*Where I'm from the dope boys is the rock stars*
*But they can't cop cars without seeing cop cars*

West rhymes "cop cars" with "cop cars," which seems lazy until you hear the way one is a verb with a direct object, and the other is an adjective describing a noun. In the first instance he's referring to stealing or owning cars, and in the second he's referring to the arrival of the police and their enforcement of the law. Even though the words are the same, their meanings couldn't be more distinct. Here's another example from Jay-Z's verse on the remix of West's "Diamonds from Sierra Leone":

> *I'm not a businessman; I'm a business, man!*
> *Let me handle my business, damn*

It's the same word again, but inserting that comma changes the meaning. In one line he's talking about doing business. In the other he's talking about being a business. When you catch the difference in the repetition, the meaning leaps out. Some dismiss the use of homonyms as lazy lyricism, and it certainly can be, but a skilled emcee can use them just like any other linguistic tool. "Rap," Adam Bradley writes, "like oral poetry through the ages, goes by the ear rather than by the book." If it sounds good, it's good.

Our minds enjoy the limits that rhymes present. They give our imagination a safe space to explore, a set of parameters established and expectations fulfilled. By using rhyme as the dominant linguistic structure, emcees hack our brains' love of harmony and heightened meaning.

### Let the Rhythm Hit 'Em

Second to rhyme, the most obvious aspect of rap is rhythm. Rhythm is what makes lyrics "hip-hop" as opposed to just words recited over a beat, and cadence is how an emcee gives their distinctive vocal signature to those lyrics. The rhythm is information. It is certainly possible to write down lyrics and study them like poetry, as many have done to great effect, but part of what makes rap unique is its rhythmic quality. Like poetry, rap contains meter, but unlike most traditional written poems, it also improvises and maintains an informal relationship with that meter. In communication theory, all forms and channels of communication technology are measured against face-to-face communication because of its richness. Thinner channels like email and text lack the richness of vocal inflection, facial expressions, and other nonverbal body language. Rap lyrics studied on the page are like the other communication channels: they are thinned-out. They're missing the layers and dynamics that make them so powerful as a performance.

In addition, the intimate and intricate relationship that the rhyme has with the beat creates new layers of rhythm. Oral poetry can rhyme without rhythm, but rap can avoid rhyme and maintain a rhythm. It's all about flow. Along with an emcee's vocal tone and inflection, the way they ride the beat defines the rhythm and style of their personality and of the song itself. The stability of the beat allows emcees to explore the rhythm around it. They can stray, flirt with falling behind, and come back, improvising new syncopations and structures. This interplay of percussion and pronunciation, rhythm and chaos is another way in which hip-hop is like jazz. An experienced emcee can sway and jam like a jazz player, alternately riding the beat like a rail and like something to be tamed.

"You know the rhythm, the rhyme, plus the beat is designed so I can enter your mind," Chuck D raps on Public Enemy's "Rebel Without a Pause." Rhythm hacks our brains because, like rhyme, our minds enjoy structure as much as surprise. A great emcee can play with both rhythm and rhyme and use them together to embed their messages in our heads.

## *Use Your Allusion*

In the early 1990s, "Uncle Tom's Cabin" was a song on the radio and *Lois & Clark* was a show on television. Those names should sound familiar independent of their popularity at that time. As if Harriet Beecher Stowe hadn't been through enough, Los Angeles hair-metal band Warrant hi-jacked the name of her most famous novel for a narrative rock song about someone witnessing a cop participating in a double murder at a cabin belonging to someone's uncle named Tom. The abolitionist themes of the novel that helped set off the Civil War were lost with the burden.

*Lois & Clark: The New Adventures of Superman* is named after its two main characters, Lois Lane and Clark Kent. The title also plays on the Lewis and Clark Expedition lead by Meriwether Lewis and William Clark. It was the first such expedition to reach the Pacific coast of the United States and established Lewis and Clark as the most instantly recognizable names of any expedition leaders in American history.

These are but two examples of media allusions. Appropriations like these hack our brains by seeming both familiar and new simultaneously. They can be as frustrating as they are effective. Some may see them as a nightmare, as the ever-encroaching co-opting of authentic experience, but to many individuals, references like this are not only familiar, they're fun. Cultural allusions invoke game play. They create a quizzical situation. To understand the reference is to be in on the gag. "It's like when I used to listen to Rakim," Tricky says, "it was like, 'fucking hell, *that's* what he means!' It's like a little game you can get involved with [...] A lot of it is the words, the way they're put down." Our media is so saturated with allusions that we scarcely think about them. A viewing of any single episode of popular television shows, seeing any big movie, or listening to any hit song yields references to any number of past cultural artifacts.

Allusions activate two texts at once, thus bringing to mind more than what they say on the surface. Rap lyrics are rife with allusions to other songs in the canon, as well as other media artifacts. These allusions give the oral history of hip-hop music a cohesion similar to that created by the musical riffs of other live instrumental-based genres.

Some consider the interpolation of lyrics an act of plagiarism. Others see such a move as metaphorical and central to the art form and indeed to historical African-American oral traditions. Remember the essential tension here: in the use of allusive appropriation in hip-hop, a practitioner must make something new while still adhering to the traditions of hip-hop. In this way, lyrical allusions can be viewed a lot like the musical samples over which they're spoken. It is often difficult to tell on which side of the line a lyric, a song, or an artist falls. The listener is often the one who must resolve the tension between innovation and imitation because rap itself is always in the middle. The tension has been around since the beginning of recorded rap. The lyrics to the Sugarhill Gang's 1979 hit, "Rapper's Delight," were lifted straight from the streets. The fact that those verses belonged originally to Grandmaster Caz and the Cold Crush Brothers is one of the oldest bits of rap lore. David Drake writes, "Hip-hop, an art poised in the balance between repetition and novelty, is really an oral tradition. The purpose of rhymes are to freeze that which is temporal and ephemeral, creating patterns and imprinting them in the cultural memory." One person's clever quip is another's cliché. Novelty is as cognitive as it is cultural.

Specific cultural allusions outside of hip-hop abound as well. Though sometimes allusions to current events or cartoons are used as punch-lines, allusions are usually used to bolster the persona of the emcee or his or her DJ. For instance, Ice-T once said that his DJ "cut like Jason," an allusion to his DJ cutting up records like Jason Vorhees cut up his victims in the *Friday the 13th* movies. Allusions to the movie *Scarface* (and indeed the Houston rapper named Scarface) have been a mainstay in rap lyrics. Here's an example that illustrates not only the power of allusions but also the layers stacked within the lyrics that bear them. This bar is from Talib Kweli on Black Star's song "Respiration":

*Killers Born Naturally, like Mickey and Mallory*
*Not knowing the ways'll get you capped, like an NBA salary*

The first line uses a reference to Oliver Stone's 1994 movie *Natural Born Killers* and its main characters to describe the way that socioeconomic conditions in the ghetto create criminals. The second line pivots on the word "capped." It means getting shot, but it's also a reference to salary limitations placed on professional basketball players. These references not only hack our individual memories, adding a layer of meaning and making them stick in our heads, but they also subvert pieces of the dominant culture, hijacking their meanings as well.

## *Allusions of Grandeur*

Henry Louis Gates, Jr. writes, "Rap's signature characteristic is the parody and pastiche of its lyrics, including 'sampling', which is another word for intertextuality." Rap lyrics are not merely intertextual though. Their interactions are far more granular. They may involve allusions to multiple, otherwise unrelated texts. In its original conception, intertextuality was considered the viewing of *one* text in terms of another. Allusions cut across texts and their genres and forms to make connections that are more than just intertextual. Allusions often include the adaptation of key phrases and proper names from other forms of mass media. Allusion is a broader literary form than parody, language that alludes to recognizable, iconic, or other shared media. Allusion here differs from intertextuality in its specificity. Some see allusion as a specific form of intertextuality. In addition, the term "intertextuality" is often misused and abused. As originally conceived by Julia Kristeva in 1966, the term meant "the transposition of one or more *systems* of signs into another." Therefore, while rap lyrics, media allusions, and conversational sampling can all be considered intertextual, their intertextuality does not indicate a cohesive system of signs. They require a more granular, specific unit for study. Using allusion to designate such a reference avoids much of the ambiguity surrounding intertextuality.

Identifying others with similar knowledge in order to establish or maintain a sense of belonging and community is an important use of figurative language in general and allusion in particular. An audience member's experience with a text is always informed by her past experience, especially past media experience, but when her experience is directly referenced with an allusion, she feels a closer experience with the text. Often, an individual will feel part of the text, as a co-creator.

The specificity of allusion is also imperative to the hacking sense of hip-hop. For example, in his 2000 song "The Way I Am," Eminem says,

*I am whatever you say I am*
*If I wasn't, then why would I say I am?*

His words have their direct meaning in response to his treatment in the media, but they also allude to a rap song from 1987: "As the Rhyme Goes On" by Eric B. & Rakim. In the earlier song, Rakim raps,

*I'm the R to the A to the K-I-M*
*If I wasn't, then why would I say I am?*

Allusions like this pose a communicative problem in that they employ and require shared knowledge. Like knowing the Linda Lee character from Gibson's *Neuromancer* was based on a character by the same name in a Velvet Underground song, at least a passing familiarity with the Eric B. & Rakim song interpolated here heightens Eminem's meaning, gives it another layer of significance and signification, and connects it to its hip-hop lineage. If you don't know the Rakim lyric, you're not in on the reference. You get left out.

In art class in high school, a friend of mine did a pencil drawing of a tree. Among its limbs he hid the phrase "no future" from the Sex Pistols song, "God Save the Queen." Our teacher, not seeing the words, told him some of his limbs had problems and that he needed to fix them. When we hear lyrics with references we don't recognize, it's like my high-school art teacher not seeing the hidden messages in the limbs of a tree drawing. Something might seem slightly off, missing, or out of place, but we're not quite sure what it is. Whereas if we catch the reference, we can see the message in the tree. An allusion like this is a great way to nod to your network and a great place to hide information from your enemies.

### Subversive Scripts

Obfuscation is the use of ambiguous, confusing, or deliberately misleading information in a public context where hiding it away is not an option. The lines blur here, but obfuscation is different from complete concealment. Privacy is not secrecy, but they're so closely related that the former seems to be lost in the fight against the latter. They're also so close as to be constantly conflated when debated. It can be a lot more technically complex than just encoding a message for a certain audience. It's like masking something without wearing a mask.

Using allusions as a game or a puzzle is not limited to television shows, movies, and music. Users employ these tactics online as a form of "social steganography." That is, hiding encoded messages where no one is likely to be looking for them: right out in the open. In one study, a teen user has problems with her mother commenting on her status updates. She finds it an invasion of her privacy, and her mom's eagerness to intervene squelches the online conversations she has with her friends. When she broke up with her boyfriend, she wanted to express her feelings to her friends but without alarming her mother. Instead of posting her feelings directly, she posted lyrics from "Always Look on the Bright Side of Life." Not knowing the allusion, her mom thought she was having a good day. Knowing that the song is from the 1979 Monty Python movie, *Life of Brian*, and that it is sung while the characters are being crucified, her friends knew that all was not well and texted her to find out what was going on.

Taking the concept a bit deeper, some argue that the individual subject is constituted by linguistic acts, rather than by nature or biology. Judith Butler is one such theorist. She points out though that being constituted by discourse is not the same as being determined by it. According to Butler, a subject who is a product of discourse can act by appropriating words in ways that imbue them with new meanings. Through these linguistic tactics, the subject can resist the dominant structures of meaning that define her and her world.

By employing obscure allusions and casting the mainstream as the out-group, a textual community like the ones found within hip-hop culture can foster cohesion and communicate via their own resistant codes. Alienating anyone outside the group strengthens the group and the barrier between inside and out. It could be as simple as using a different vocabulary, a code like referring to men as Gods and women as Earths, which are aspects of the language of the Five Percent Nation, a group who provide another excellent example of allusive resistance.

The Five Percent Nation, or the Nation of Gods and Earths, is a splinter sect of the Nation of Islam started by Clarence Smith a.k.a. Clarence 13X in the early 1960s. Though they reject any associations with the religion of Islam, the Five-Percenter worldview is based on an amalgam of traditional Nation of Islam doctrines, Masonic mysticism, Kemetic imagery, and peculiar spatial knowledge of the Earth and planets. From Rakim to RZA, many popular rappers identify themselves as a part of this group and use allusions to its teachings in their songs. For instance, in the song "Triumph" by the Wu-Tang Clan, Masta Killa rhymes,

*Ninety-three million miles away from came one*
*To represent the Nation*

He is claiming to be a chosen one of God, as the Sun, which represents God in Five Percent Nation teachings, is ninety-three million miles away from the earth. If one doesn't know the doctrine, then one is left out of the message. Allusions to Five-Percent Nation lessons deliberately create a distinctive in-group and out-group, what a Five Percenter would call a *cipher*. "Brief references [to Five Percenter theology] in the midst of otherwise standard rap fare," Miyakawa writes, "serve as momentary nods to those already initiated..." Earlier in the same song, RZA raps,

*March of the wooden soldiers*
*C-Cypher-Punks couldn't hold us*

Here RZA likens the Wu-Tang Clan to the unstoppable, inexhaustible army of wooden soldiers in the 1934 Laurel and Hardy movie, *Babes in Toyland*, which is also known as *March of the Wooden Soldiers*. "C-Cypher-Punks" is code for the police. Using the Roman alphabet, the Supreme Alphabet, and a sly pejorative, RZA spells out "cops," adding that they aren't able to stop the Clan. These allusive expressions are not particularly inviting or instructive to those in the outgroup. As allusions so often are, they are alienating and confusing, representing an act of resistance against mainstream culture and society at large.

These coded messages are hiding out loud. Oppression never completely silences the voices of the oppressed. Rather, discourses that would be controversial in the dominant public sphere are obscured, preserved in code. James C. Scott calls these *hidden transcripts*. In a rhetorical environment of domination, powerless groups voice their resistance in coded forms: "The theatrical imperatives that normally prevail in situations of domination produce a public transcript in close conformity with how the dominant group would wish to have things appear [...] the hidden transcript takes place off-stage." Hip-hop lyrics are heavy with hidden transcripts against police brutality, systemic racism, and other oppressive forces. These tactics are even used among factions waging battle beyond the attention of the larger culture. Gangs fight over territory and turf, graffiti artists paint over each other's pieces, and rival rappers appropriate each other's lyrics and defile each other's instrumentals. However, many acts of resistance are a matter of negotiating barriers or borders rather than reinforcing them.

## Boundary Functions

Allusions, quotations, metaphors, and other figurative expressions provide the points at which multiple texts, genres, and groups connect. They are where textual communities compare notes. These overlapping edges are also where hip-hop hacks the surrounding culture. Barry Brummett sums up the situation nicely when he writes,

> Texts are complex and polysemous, both discrete and diffuse. They are nodal: what one experiences here and now is a text, but it may well be a part of a larger text extending into time and space. Texts tend to grow nodes off themselves into larger, more complex but re- lated texts. The texts we present to others by which they read us are likely to extend in time and space and to be a part of larger political and social texts in which one personally does not appear... This is especially true of a rhetoric of style, which is a continuous series of nodal displays and readings scattered throughout everyday life and media and linked to other nodes of texts created by other people and groups.

The practitioners and fans of subcultures like hip-hop represent what Etienne Wenger calls *communities of practice*. These are communities united by similar goals, practices, and vocabularies. Boundary objects aid communication between these communities by translating differences. Boundary objects can be words, concepts, metaphors, allusions, artifacts, and other nodes around which communities organize their overlaps and interconnections. These connective terms emphasize groups' similarities rather than their differences, as opposed to the social steganography discussed above. Allusions and other linguistic forms act as boundary objects between different communities of practice, hacking borders once inaccessible, circulating ideas into alien territories.

"Just as graffiti writers hitched a ride on the subways and used its power to distribute their tags," Tricia Rose writes, "rappers 'hijacked' the market for their own purposes." Practicing another aspect of hip-hop culture, graffiti artists reanimate and repurpose the walls of the city and the cars of trains. They didn't wait for permission from curators to show their work. Long before it became fashionable to "disrupt" markets and industries, aerosol artists turned the traditional gallery structure onside out, displaying their work directly to the public, on, in, and near the trains and other hi-traffic areas. No filters. Moving both inward and outward, they hack not just words and language but the letters themselves.

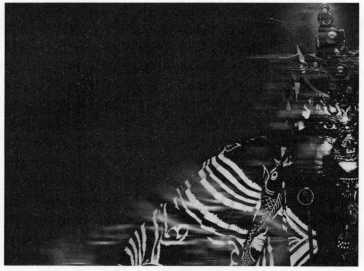
The Equation: Rammellzee. Photo by Timothy Saccenti.

## Chapter Five

# THE PROCESS OF ILLUMINATION

"Gothic's obsession with decay, and its tradition of political negativity, makes it at the end of the twentieth century an aesthetic of defacement. It produces graffiti — sometimes uncouth, in other instances witty or intelligent — defying or decrying complacently rationalistic social controls which, though ostensibly intended to restore an idealistic humanist harmony, actually enforce a regime of trivialized sameness."
— Richard Davenport-Hines, *Gothic: Four Hundred Years of Excess, Horror, Evil and Ruin*

"From the moment commodified Africans realized their very thoughts could violate the delusions of white exceptionalism, the physics of the owners' universe began to disintegrate."
— Greg Tate, *Flyboy 2*

"Darkness has its own sanctuary. Blade runners of the masonry. We who have been trained in the unbelievable stationery with a word that describes us as peasants. I command legends whether it be son of the father, ghosts of the holler, without cost their description is non-ethical, but perplexable."
— Rammellzee, *The Art of Terrorism*

While the Gothic as a genre of fiction is marked by the dark, the grotesque, by a kludging together of elements, it also refers to a style of lettering. "The Romans stole the alphabeta system from the Greeks through war," writes hip-hop pioneer and graffiti philosopher Rammellzee, "Then in medieval times, monks ornamented letters to hide their meaning from the people. Now, the letter is armored against further manipulation." As the posters for his 2018 Red Bull Academy retrospective read, "If This Knowledge Scares You, The Equation is Working."

Before we get into Rammellzee and his theory of Gothic Futurism, let's back up. Sometimes the way to the future is back through the past.

### Set the Controls for the Heart of the Sun

In making Public Enemy's loud and chaotic, Frankenstein soundscapes, Chuck D describes the Bomb Squad's early jam sessions with turntables, drum machines, samplers, and sequencers like those of a band: "all four of us would just be playing." Various blinking machines all blasting noise, most of it was a mess, he admits, but sometimes magic happened: "That was the closest thing to a jazz band you could have, just jamming. Maybe not a conventional jazz band. Maybe someone like Sun Ra." Producer Ed Michel describes his first Sun Ra mixing session in 1972 similarly:

> At that point I liked to mix at the pain threshold. It was really loud. We were mixing it quadraphonically in a relatively small room. Sun Ra was sleeping deep and

snoring loud. For some reason, I stopped the tape in the middle of the tune. He came awake, wheeled his head like an owl does — all around the room, checking everything out. He said, "You Earth people sleep too much." He put his head down and started to snore again.

Interplanetary immigrant Sun Ra, who arrived here as Herman Poole Blount in Birmingham, Alabama in 1914, was the most prolific recording artist of the twentieth century. The stories vary — it would be more surprising if they didn't — but he was allegedly named after the magician Black Herman. The most famous African-American magician of his time, Black Herman also served as the basis for the character of the same name in Ishmael Reed's 1972 novel *Mumbo Jumbo*. Herman, which in Ancient Germanic means *soldier*, created a backstory that detailed his African origins and claimed that his magic tricks were leftover Zulu survival strategies against colonialism.

In the 1950s, Sun Ra migrated to Chicago and joined the jazz scene. There he adopted his alien name and persona, abandoning his ties to Earth. He claimed to be from Saturn, and his music, art, and writings were all created as such. He rejected mainstream society and consensus reality, opting instead for the power and vision of his own art. Sun Ra rejected white hegemony for creative black heresy.

The most recent book on Sun Ra's life and legacy, Paul Youngquist's *A Pure Solar World: Sun Ra and the Birth of Afrofuturism* (2017) establishes Sun Ra as a germinal deity in the pantheon of Afrofuturist gods. Not since John F. Szwed's *Space is the Place* (1997) and the first two chapters of

Graham Lock's *Blutopia* (1999) has there been an in-depth study of Sun Ra that connects as many dots as Younquist's. While most studies of Afrofuturism trace its roots at least back to Sun Ra, studies of Sun Ra don't necessarily make such an explicit connection to his Afrofuturist legacy: Szwed mentions the word once; Lock doesn't use the term at all. These can't be viewed as oversights, as Sun Ra returned home to Saturn around the same time the term was first used. Baltimore emcee Labtekwon put the disjunction to me this way:

> I never heard Sun Ra or George Clinton use the term "Afrofuturism", and they inspired me to imagine an ancient future since I was a child. To be honest, I am not even sure if Octavia Butler ever used the term either, but I think poser culture takes elements of real cultural paradigms and makes weak clones for mass consumption.

Contention has followed the term since its emergence in 1993, and so far, its lineage is longer than its legacy. Labtekwon continues:

> [T]he legacy of Black people envisioning the future is ancient in itself. When we see the Dogon people predicting the return of Nibiru for thousands of years or the nature of Nile Valley civilization and interdimensional relationships, this idea of imagining and projecting into the future existed long before the term "Afrofuturism" [...] My interest in science fiction as a Black child is 100% connected to the ancient legacy of my people.

So, for me "Afrofuturism" is a cliché, but it can be used to describe authentic aspects of Black culture and art.

Afrofuturism also addresses the neglect of the Black Diaspora not only historically but also in science-fiction visions of the future. "They had a movie of the future called *Logan's Run*?" Sun Ra once wrote, noting the lack of black people. "I said, 'Well, white folks ain't planning for us to be here!'" The core assumption of Afrofuturism is that the apocalypse has already happened. As Sun Ra told his audience at Soundscape in New York in 1979, "You've outlived the Bible, which was your scenario," adding that we're living "in a science fiction film now." Like his Afrofuturist progeny, instead of retrofitting Black lives into an outmoded history, Sun Ra was writing a new one. As Rammellzee once said, "I believe the first spaceship is a steeple."

This is our story now, a storm blowing us backwards into the future, where revisions gone by and visions yet to come become part of the same process, where slave narratives and science-fiction stories find common ground in their conflicting histories and spin off into new futures. As Lock puts it,

[...] just as the slaves "sacred world" brought together past and future, space and time, in the eternal now of the ring shout, so Sun Ra united ancient Egypt and outer space in his myth-world and celebrated the union in his sacred arena, the concert, where costumes and instruments alike linked the worlds of Africa and science fiction, and the entire spectrum of black creative music was enacted in ceremonious and colorful spectacle.

The African-American experience is inherently one of alienation, in which the African Diaspora are living a science-fiction story just by coming and being in America. Slave trade seen as alien abduction has become another Afrofuturist cliché.

Just as traditional science fiction privileges the white race over others, cyberpunk often does as well. With its Off-World colonies as space-borne suburbs to the gentrification of the planet Earth, *Blade Runner* can be read this way. The races are separated enough to prompt one of the Replicants to ask a white character why he hasn't moved Off-World, as most white people have left the deteriorating planet to the "inferior" races. He is physically unable, having a disorder that speeds his aging. Commiserating with her as a Replicant with a finite lifespan, he calls his predicament "accelerated decrepitude." Ruth Wilson Gilmore writes that racism is "the state-sanctioned and/or extra-legal production and exploitation of group-differentiated vulnerabilities to premature death." That's the racist regime's fail-safe against Replicants and the less desirable races: a limited lifespan, a limited life.

Closer to home, while most were celebrating Neil Armstrong and Buzz Aldrin's jaunt to the moon in 1969, jazz poet and proto-rapper Gil Scott-Heron used the occasion to highlight racial disparities here on Earth. The song "Whitey on the Moon" includes the verses,

*I can't pay no doctor bills*
*But Whitey's on the moon*
*Ten years from now I'll be paying still*
*While Whitey's on the moon*

*You know, The Man just upped my rent last night*
*'Cause Whitey's on the moon*
*No hot water, no toilets, no lights*
*But Whitey's on the moon*

Looking back even further, the conspiratorial view of ancient aliens or astronauts has racism at its roots as well. It's easier for people to believe that aliens came to Earth, built pyramids, created artifacts, and taught early humans language and mathematics than it is for them to believe that Egyptians had their own advanced society long before white Europeans. There are several theories, but the most popular version was put forth by Erich von Däniken in his 1968 book *Chariots of the Gods?* The basic premise ponders whether the primitive gods unearthed by modern archaeology were actually alien visitors. How else could these ancient alien artifacts exist? The book set off a spate of similar speculation: Andrew Tomas's *We Are Not the First* (1971), Jacques Bergier's *Extraterrestrial Visitations from Prehistoric Times to the Present* (1973), Alan and Sally Landsburg's *In Search of Ancient Mysteries* (1974), and von Däniken's own follow-ups *Gods from Outer Space* (1971) and *The Gold of the Gods* (1972), among many others. One such book, *The Spaceships of Ezekiel* (1974), written by NASA engineer Josef F. Blumrish, uses the Bible to support von Däniken's original claims of paleocontact.

Unlike most of these ancient alien theorists, Robert Charroux explicitly insinuates race into his theories. Charroux claimed that the pale race that once dominated the whole world in the ancient past was extraterrestrial in origin. According to Charroux's 1974 book *The Mysterious*

*Past*, these white folks had originally come from a cold planet far from our sun. Filling in gaps in history and extant mysteries, these texts and subsequent television shows ask over and over again whether ancient sites like Stonehenge, the pyramids, or the Nazca Lines were messages from early humans to their alien ancestors or breadcrumbs the visitors left to find their way back. Their specious speculations also retrofit stories that benefit those in power, while revising histories to do the same.

Similarly, contemporary monastic think-tanks, studying and deliberating futures, are funded by corporations and governments eager for an edge on the oncoming. Anything that gives power or voice or hope to the Other threatens that edge. Eshun writes,

> The powerful employ futurists and draw power from the futures they endorse, thereby condemning the disempowered to live in the past. The present moment is stretching, slipping for some into yesterday, reaching for others into tomorrow.

As much as the music of Sun Ra, Lee "Scratch" Perry, George Clinton, Rammellzee, and Afrika Bambataa, and the writing of Samuel R. Delany, Octavia Butler, Alondra Nelson, and Kodwo Eshun, these restless roots of history begat the tenets and terms of Afrofuturism. Whether gentrified or by genocide, the future as seen by traditional science-fiction authors and ancient astronaut theorists might be full of aliens, but it does not include black people. As skeptical as it is speculative, Afrofuturism has come as a corrective to that.

## Saucer Wisdom

The first widely cited UFO sighting in the United States occurred in Seattle in 1947. Idaho pilot Kenneth Arnold spotted nine saucers flying in formation near Mount Rainier, thereby naming them "flying saucers." Roughly fifty years later, science-fiction author Octavia Butler moved to the Seattle area. Now the home of the Space Needle hosts the spaced-out sounds of Shabazz Palaces. As much as I argue that all of hip-hop is the sound of the future, some groups are more deliberately so. As mentioned above, the history of the genre so far can be seen as split down the middle by the deaths of Biggie Smalls and Tupac Shakur. In the most oversimplified of terms, there was a reset in the mid-1990s when street sounds gave way to club bangers. Wu-Tang and Nas stepped aside for Missy and Puffy. Few survived.

Ishmael Butler has been on both sides of that divide. His old New York crew, Digable Planets, was all over the place in the early 1990s. Along with similar tracks by A Tribe Called Quest and Gang Starr, their Grammy award-winning song "Rebirth of Slick (Cool Like Dat)" inadvertently solidified jazz-rap as a subgenre. Butler's new Seattle outfit with Tendai "Baba" Maraire, Shabazz Palaces, is firmly a part of the future, though he doesn't necessarily see time and space like that. Time and space, like reality itself, are human constructs. "Every serious artist hopes not to be a success but to escape the gravity, the pull, the prison of their times," Charles Mudede tells me. "Ish, I think, is the only rapper who achieved escape velocity and is now free in space."

Shabazz Palaces: Ishmael Butler and Tendai Maraire.
Photo by Victoria Kovios.

Of the 1993 Digable Planets song "Time & Space (A New Refutation of)," Butler says,

That song title was part of the title of the album. It came from Jorge Luis Borges. I was reading a lot of his stuff at the time [...] Everything he wrote was metaphysical and circular, and things didn't always happen for any reason. Time and space are conceptual and can only relate to you as an individual.

After having released one of the most overlooked records in the history of music, 1994's *Blowout Comb* (Pendulum), Digable Planets split up in the mid-1990s. They haven't recorded any new material since, but they've been performing live again since 2005. Shabazz Palaces is still Butler's main focus though.

Thoroughly informed by science fiction — *Z for Zachariah* was the first book Butler ever read all the way through — Shabazz Palaces find inspiration in the deep past and the far future. Like Sun Ra before them, they explore themes from both ancient Egypt and interstellar space. After a quick mention of Octavia Butler, George Clinton is Ish Butler's next reference. "I don't really call that science fiction," he says, "I call it imaginative reality [...] where you exist because you believe in different realms, different worlds, natural words, supernatural worlds [...] these alternative realities different from ours but no less real. I came onto that early in life." I asked him for his thoughts on Afrofuturism, and they're well worth quoting at length:

> I like the alien aspect of it only because white people were the first to construct this reality that was concrete, had reason and had form and hierarchies and categories and you could understand everything, you know? That just wasn't something that African motherfuckers were concerned with. We didn't need to lord over the land and the air and the space and ideas and people — not to that extent. So, when those that did came into contact with us and saw us, that was the birth of science fiction. This notion of a reality and that we had broken that reality therefore set into motion all these needs

to put hierarchies and to control and to enslave and to have land and borders and all of this kind of stuff. I feel like we are the alien. We deal with this realm in a totally different way than anyone else. And I think that it's shocking and disorienting and calls into question reality... It blew people away and it set into motion all of these things like science fiction and abstraction and cubism and surrealism and all that stuff. I feel like we were catalysts to all of that stuff just by our existence. I look at Towers in Luxor or the Pyramids or different types of structures, and I'm like, yeah, there was some different type of shit going on. I don't think anyone knew what it was, and there are all kinds of theories that are interesting and entertaining and brilliantly conceived, but no one really knows... Something else was happening! It appears obvious to me. I hear that when [George] Clinton and those guys get down, when Prince gets down... There's something else at work in these constructions that these people are making.

Frantz Fanon maintained that the alien is not defined by the alien itself, that the Other is always othered from the outside, and usually in pejorative terms. It is also in this way that racism precedes race. If one needs to "lord over the land and the air and the space and ideas and people," the first thing one needs to do is name and categorize those things. The Other or the alien is put down only after it is named, and contemporary media representations tell us more about the dominant cultural attitudes and anxieties than they do about the antecedents of those representations. Marketing marginalizes artists while it targets consumers.

Acts are corralled into categories based on audience appeal instead of artistic merit. Art and activities are called alien if they threaten the norms of polite society. It's the difference between a billboard bought in the daylight and a mural painted in the dark.

Shabazz Palaces: *Quazarz: Born on a Gangster Star*.

### Tales from the Rails

"The graffiti on the subway cars has evolved during the two years I've been in Germany," Rudy Rucker writes, returning to New York City in the late 1980s, "You can't read the names at all anymore. The wild abstract expressionist 'lettering' covers all the windows so you just have to know where to get out." When pressed about his motivation for writing graffiti in the 1983 documentary *Style Wars*, graffiti artist Dust explains that the elder writers give you a name and tell you to see how big you can get it. "They give you a name, and they say, 'Here, take this name and do something with it'," he explains. "'How big could you get this name up? How high?'" Branding and advertising are charged with similar motivation and similar challenges. Corporations pay large consulting fees and individual fame-seekers flaunt themselves online for the same reasons. As Jelani Cobb puts it, "Long before low-wattage celebrities thought to brand or cross-promote themselves, artists were rapping and tagging graffiti under the same alias as to ensure that one's rep received its maximum dissemination." Greg Tate adds, "Their efforts paved the way not only for hip-hop as an artform but also for the scale of commodification and self-promotion that defines today's hip-hop."

Companies develop — or hire other companies to develop — brand identities and campaigns. Logos, slogans, and thematic series of ads combine to sell products, to garner brand recognition, and eventually to maintain brand loyalty. Graffiti tags have to be catchy, and they have to have good letters — letters that can be twisted up and together in wild style forms often only legible to other writers. "I don't care about nobody else seeing it," says Skeme in *Style Wars*, "or the fact if they can read it or not. It's for me and other graffiti writers, that we can read it. These other people who don't write, they're excluded. I don't care about them, you know? They don't matter to me. It's for us." Like the obscure allusions in rap lyrics, graffiti is often deliberately divisive.

Graffiti, and its corporate-sanctioned sister, advertising, are our modern-day cave paintings. As McLuhan once put it, "[…] ads are not intended to be seen but to produce an <u>effect</u>. The cave paintings were carefully hidden. They were a magic form, intended to affect events at a distance. They were of corporate, not private origin." With graffiti, one tries to get a name as big as one can, as many places as one can, and in the most unique style. The name, the style, the aesthetics are not for anyone but members of the graffiti culture. This most public of art is not meant for the public. "Ours was a world where acknowledgment from one's peers was the singularly ultimate gratification," explains graffiti legend Phase 2. "Never has there been an urgency to be accepted by the public or anyone else." As emcee KRS-One puts it on his 1995 song, "Out for Fame,"

*Historically speakin', 'cause people be dissin'*
*The first graffiti artists in the world were the Egyptians*
*Writing on the walls, mixing characters with letters*
*To tell the graphic story about their life, however*
*Today we do the same thing, with how we rap and draw*
*We call it hardcore, they call it breakin' the law*

KRS-One draws a connection similar to the one McLuhan drew above. Like Gladys Glover in the 1954 film, *It Should Happen to You*, where Gladys seeks fame at all cost, buying up billboards all over the city, graffiti artists and advertisers emblazon their names wherever eyeballs may light. Not content with being part of the crowd, they want to be above the crowd. It's all about building a name. Advertising is only effective at making brand impressions, and graffiti is written in a code only decipherable by its practitioners. The painted caves are all around us, their notes are noise with rarely received signals, barely residual effects, hidden transcripts on every suitable surface.

Brands and their logos are modern-day sigils intended to affect actions from afar. Their effects are subliminal at best, nonexistent at worst. The ubiquity of advertising makes it invisible. It's wallpaper. It's cliché. It's the Post-It Note that's still on your monitor from months ago, signifying something long since passed, thereby signifying nothing. That is why companies are trying everything they can think of to get our attention. In places where the spray can rules the walls, graffiti disappears as well. It's just there, without effect. Unless you're a graffiti writer, it's just not directly a part of your world, not unlike the way that bus routes are invisible to drivers, but very much a part of the bus-rider's daily life. It's ambient imagery.

As McLuhan put it, "The magic of the cave image lies in its *being*, not in its being seen. The symbolic does not refer. It *is*."

### Remixed Relics

Alpha-Positive, a secretary known as Vain the Insane, a maître d' called Chaser the Eraser, Ripcord Rex, Crux the Monk, Vocal Wells God a.k.a. Chimer the Galactic Bookie, Duchess of Candor, Shun-U the Loan Sharker, Destiny Destiny, Wind the Mother of Natures, Reaper Grim, a pimp named Barshaw Gangstarr, a judge named Igniter the Master Alphabiter, Evolution Griller the Master Killer: these are characters in a science-fiction saga, a few of the many guises of graffiti philosopher, performance artist, black cyberpunk, Rammellzee. These battle-borne B-boys are demigods in a gothic-futurist mythology, post-catastrophe cosplay in an aerosol-art universe. Rammellzee was from another world, like his stylistic godfather Sun Ra. "They are in the vein of African power sculptures," Greg Tate writes of Rammellzee's constructions, "assemblages with hidden powers and meanings waiting to be activated by their builders and makers."

"Rammellzee is alien material," Ish Butler says. "My man was from another place. We might never know where it was, but it ain't here!" Rammellzee legally changed his name to a mathematical equation. From what? "It is not to be told. That is forbidden," his late wife said.

One of the originators of graffiti steganography, wild-style lettering legible only to the enlightened, Rammellzee emerged from the train tunnels of New York City in the late 1970s. Like many of his contemporaries, Rammellzee was a Renaissance B-boy: he wrote graffiti, performed, acted, emceed, and cobbled together elaborate scriptures, sculptures, and costumes out of the discarded scraps of the city. He was able to freestyle for hours on esoteric topics like thermodynamics, astrophyiscs, typography, and linguistics. He explained graffiti, his and others, to higher levels of knowledge and understanding. Fab 5 Freddy describes him as "part street physics professor, part trickster." He appeared in both germinal graffiti movies, *Wild Style* and *Style Wars*. His 1983 single with K-Rob, "Beat Bop," on which he is widely credited with innovating the high-pitched, nasal vocal style adopted by the Beastie Boys, B-Real of Cypress Hill, and Detroit's Danny Brown, a style he called "Gangsta Duck," was funded, illustrated, and "produced" by Jean-Michel Basquiat. Al Diaz, who played percussion on the record, says, "Rammellzee was the Sun Ra of hip hop and graffiti." The single is a certified classic of early recorded hip-hop, and the 12" sells for thousands of dollars. Though his other records get less attention, they're all worth a listen for their ability to sound simultaneously old-school and wildly futuristic. "Rammellzee is on purpose," says Bootsy Collins. "He is a speck of magic galaxy dust from another time." Rammellzee considered Sun Ra, George Clinton, the Hells Angels, AC/DC, and Gene Simmons all among his forebears.

Rammellzee: Alfa A with Harpoon Extendor.

Of all the roles he played, Rammellzee was perhaps above all a semiotic soldier: "I see that society is using all they can use [standard English] to define their own history. I use

what I use to define mine. I build a letter like a weapon."
Graffiti is a tradition of resistance, and there was no one
more militant than Rammellzee. "The piece itself became
a weapon: the letter itself," he wrote, "The letter is armed
to stop all the phony formations, lies, and tricknowlegies
placed upon its structure. You think war is always shooting
and beating everybody, but no, we had the letters fight
for us." Rammellzee explained graffiti's gothic legacy as a
rediscovery of the Gothic illuminated alphabet:

> The graffiti artists of the 1970s in the tunnels of New
> York continued where the monks of the fourteenth
> century had left off with their illuminated letters. Back
> then handwritten religious scripts were the main way
> to spread any form of knowledge. Those monks, who
> were fighting with the clerical elite, started to decorate
> the letters with ornamental outlines so they could illu-
> minate the truth in the core of the letters. These letters
> are electromagnetic structures and as fonts they repre-
> sent pure knowledge. In order to protect this knowl-
> edge, the monks sent the letters to a place where the
> clerical elite wouldn't dare to go: hell. That's where
> they stayed until, in the early 1970s, the first graffiti
> writers rediscovered them in the gothic tunnels of the
> New York transit system.

In Rammellzee's view, graffiti writers were mediums of
the monks, channeling their art and energy. "From the
fourth century to the nineteenth century," he wrote, "a
development of style remanipulated by monks known as
Gothic type, or Old English type, presently used by *The New*

*York Times* and *Long Island Press*. This is the PROTO-product of WILD-STYLING." Envisioning a war between letters and the meaning imposed upon them, he further claimed the deconstruction and militarization of the alphabet was then enabled by the secret equation RΔMM:ΣLL:ΖΣΣ. He explained the name this way:

> "RΔMM" is Raamses, the son of the Egyptian sun god; is Raham in the Black Muslim Community; is ram, meaning to batter, to be in forward motion, also the straight arrows of wild-style lettering. ΣLL is leverage, elevation, promotion. If you are ramming something and it's elevating, that means it's flying. "ΖΣΣ" [if you trace the design of a Z] is the pattern of the way we read a page.

"These are alien shapes!" Ish Butler says. "If you write your name in some crazy wild style, and you come up with this crazy shape, it's coming from your DNA. That's coming from all the things you've ever been into this one crystallized moment." Rammellzee agreed: "The genetic code of the species does not dictate past tense. It allows us to dream."

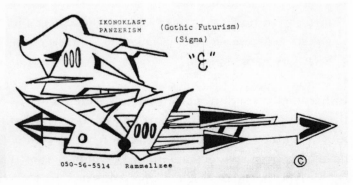

Rammellzee: Sigma E.

"All of my art and teachings are about Gothic Futurism," he said. His "Iconic Treatise on Gothic Futurism" reimagined the history of the alphabet. Separated from their linguistic functions, the letters are weapons against oppressive and fraudulent language systems. In addition to the traditions of graffiti and Gothic typography, his philosophy of Gothic Futurism is built on the Five-Percenter teachings of the Father (Clarence 13X) whom he knew personally. He continues:

We're advanced in terms of science and technology, but the attitude of the population is still Gothic. We still do not know what we're doing. We still do not know how to leave this planet the right way. We'll bring religion out into space and it'll be stopped. Because in the 1400s the word "religion" was *restriction* on a *legion*. Gothic is the architecture of the letter that was back in the fourteenth century. You can have four alternatives to human nature — genocide, plain old socialism like bees and ants have, love and dictatorship, which is what we have now, or you can have a lot of high-powered mega-structured knowledge where everything becomes not a socialistic bee-type state but a militant state with megastructures. That's the way it should be — mass thinking, mass brain power as one.

The Rammellzee thought about all things from odd angles. Anything you could do, he could do meta.

## Long Live the New Flesh

One third of the core behind the UK's late, post-progressive crew, New Flesh for Old, Juice Aleem is no stranger to the future. He tangled with the Rammellzee firsthand and came out unscarred and admired. "Meeting Ramm in person is a crazy thing..." he tells me via email, "I'd been interested in his music and art, but it wasn't till I read the Ionic Treatise that I became interested in the man and his mission." New Flesh recorded a few tracks with Rammellzee, two of which made it onto their 2002 record, *Understanding*: "His Stories Crockery" and "Mack Facts." But according to Aleem, there was so much more planned:

> There was intended to be a whole series of stories from his Cosmic opera. "Mack Facts" was cool 'cause we had a theme of this whole future arena style thing with us being the gladiators and Ramm as the announcer. Think of an intense episode of that Gwar, *Mad Max* show starring Sonny Chiba and Sho Kosugi as Nuba warriors on Plutonia. Speaking with him and listening to him so much on those tapes was kinda trippy, and how he'd take any little idea and run with it, creating a session's worth of vocals... This wasn't your average 16 bars, but reams and reams of classic adventure rasped in an intense style that fully drew you in. We still have a few bits and pieces from those sessions.

Aleem was one of the only emcees Rammellzee acknowledged outside of the old-school pioneers. And Aleem acknowledges him in kind:

Rammellzee is The Equation. Father to a lot of styles in a lot of traditions and I'm just thankful to have known and worked with him. In even the few times we met, so much wisdom was imparted it was incredible. His lineage is also the real and true artist, the gangster artist who learns and teaches by an innate skillset. He is the furthest thing from fame/art school celeb and continued on regardless to his position in the history books. This is a lesson he taught all of us.

"You call me an Afrofuturist," Rammellzee once said. "I am of the Gothics." The Gothics reject the idea of human identity as a stable entity. "Instead Goths celebrate human identity as an improvised performance, discontinuous and incessantly re-devised by stylized acts [...]" Davenport-Hines writes. "[H]uman existence is constructed out of innumerable acts of social, emotional and stylistic imitation: whether high-minded emulation, or low-grade histrionic stunts, or some intermediate form of copying." A name on a wall, a voice on a tape, identity is repetition with a difference. Identity is a performance. Identity is a haunting.

"His energy has just gone out to the Van Allen Belt, I'm sure," his late widow Carmela Zagari Rammellzee said when Rammellzee passed in 2010, "and pretty soon it's going to come back to us again."

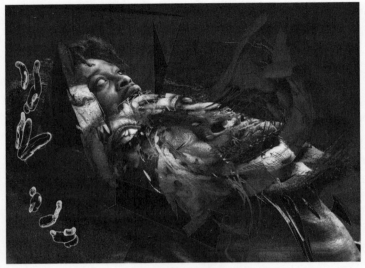

Atrocity Exhibition: Danny Brown. Photo by Timothy Saccenti.

## Chapter Six

# LET BYGONES BE ICONS

"Tape-recorders. A mechanical contrivance, a substitute for the voice; depersonalized man [sic]. The dead speak to the living; it is a mechanical ghost."
— Raymond Durgnat, *Films and Feelings*

"What used to be hot was what a emcee said,
Now hip-hop don't respect you unless you platinum or dead."
— Ras Kass, "Van Gogh"

"Anything dead coming back to life hurts."
— Amy Denver, in Toni Morrison's *Beloved*

Rammellzee left this planet in 2010. In the time since, I have read his words, listened to his music, and watched him discuss his theories in various video clips. We think nothing of reading the words of the dead, hearing their voices, or watching them in movies. We weren't always so comfortable sharing this realm with those who had passed on to another. William Gibson describes the advent of recording technology, saying,

An English clergyman had gone to a garden party, and he'd heard an Edison wax-cylinder Victrola. And he'd come home and was just completely traumatized by it [...] He said that he had heard "A voice from Hell": this "undead, hideous parody of the human voice", and that mankind was "doomed", and, "how could God let such things be?" [...] I doubt if he would've had the same reaction [...] the next time around, but this diary entry caught him [...] on the cusp of the change.

In a 1920 interview given to B.C. Forbes, the founder of *Forbes* magazine, Thomas Edison himself, who had a life-long interest in the paranormal, said the following:

If our personality survives, then it is strictly logical and scientific to assume that it retains memory, intellect, and other faculties and knowledge that we acquire on earth [...] I am inclined to believe that our personality hereafter will be able to affect matter. If this reasoning be correct, then, if we can evolve an instrument so delicate as to be affected, or moved, or manipulated — whichever term you want to use — by our personality as it survives in the next life, such an instrument, when made available, ought to record something.

One of the characters in Gibson's *Neuromancer* is a recording in a box like a tape in a portable player, similar to what Edison describes above. Dixie Flatline, so nicknamed because of his three deaths while hacking, and of course his fourth and final, used to be famous computer hacker McCoy Pauley, mentor to the main character, Case. His mind was uploaded onto a ROM chip before his last flatline, and he's now a construct in a Hosaka computer deck: "When the construct laughed, it came through as something else, not laughter, but a stab of cold down Case's spine." Like the clergyman above, hearing the voice of the dead when taken as such is still a scary thing.

### Distorted Forms

Using the studio as a vessel, many artists have envisioned recording as a journey, some to other worlds, some to other versions of themselves. Early on in his book *Decoded*, Jay-Z writes,

> The first time I heard our voices playing back on tape, I realized that a recording captures you, but plays back a distortion — a different voice from the one you hear in your own head, even though I could recognize myself instantly. I saw it as an opening, a way to re-create myself and reimagine my world.

The subtle differences between being a person and performing a persona, the possibilities and power of recording are captured in this simple insight. The space between the person and the persona is where performance does its work. It's where the ghosts of media do their haunting.

The main character in *Neuromancer*, Case, is a hacker, a "console cowboy," who is constantly trying to escape his body. His very name is a reference to his feeling trapped by his flesh. A previous employer, having caught him stealing from them, poisoned him as to make sure he wouldn't work again:

> They damaged his nervous system with a wartime Russian mycotoxin.
> Strapped to a bed in a Memphis hotel, his talent burning out micron by micron, he hallucinated for thirty hours.
> The damage was minute, subtle, and utterly effective.
> For Case, who'd lived for the bodiless exultation of cyberspace, it was the Fall. In the bars he'd frequented as a cowboy hotshot, the elite stance involved a certain relaxed contempt for the flesh. The body was meat. Case fell into the prison of his own flesh.

Other characters in the book undergo cosmetic surgeries of all kinds, modifying their bodies to look more or less Western or even animalistic. The body is the site of anxiety, not just of one's self-image but of its legality. A system, a person of power, an enemy cannot impose their law or hatred on someone with no body. Racism precedes race, and race is of the body.

Escaping race and gender, if not the body altogether, was one of the central concerns of cyberpunk and also one of the many initial dreams of the internet. Online, no one knows you're a dog or a woman or just another white dude. No one can impose their prejudices upon you if you have no body. The idea that technology will liberate us from the bounds of the body persists in spite of how things on the internet turned out. Louis Chude-Sokei writes,

It is because of this nexus of race and technology and the historical intimacy of that parallel that it is not so strange that cyberpunk fiction and film made fairly constant references and recourses to race and black music in their attempts to question or problematize the human.

Seemingly confused and conflicting influences, temporal disjunction, and general disorder are often evident in both cyberpunk and hip-hop, but they are also elements that define the Gothic. While both genres predate its publication in 1818, Mary Shelley's *Frankenstein* is widely considered one of the first novels of both the Gothic and science-fiction persuasions. Its monster remains one of the most useful and recognizable allusions in literature. Monsters like the one in the book signify other versions, worlds, or futures unrealized. And like any good hacker, Dr. Frankenstein pushes his technology past its previous limits and accepted uses.

Catherine Waldby writes, "The novel both describes and prefigures a world in which the human body and human sociality owe a greater and greater debt to technoscientific and machinic systems of production and reproduction, and are less and less able to be thought of outside of those systems." Whether those systems be textual, legal, or biological, the body is the site of our engagement with them. That this particular once-dead body is assembled and reanimated by science and technology is the difference between *Frankenstein* and the monster stories that preceded it. That's the science in this science fiction.

Hip-hop's most obvious direct connection to the Gothic

lies in its horrorcore subgenre. In the simplest of terms, horrorcore takes the violence of gangster rap and adds a layer of the supernatural, the demonic, the drug-induced, or the downright psychotic. If the song or artist gives you the same feelings or uses the same themes that typical horror movies do, then it could be considered horrorcore. The subgenre is also burdened with the same controversies that surround movies of this kind. There are horrorcore elements in rap songs as far back as 1980's "Adventures of Super Rhyme," in which Jimmy Spicer unveils a tale of meeting Dracula to sportscaster Howard Cosell. Dana Dane rapped about his bad dreams in "Nightmares." DJ Jazzy Jeff and the Fresh Prince had a hit in 1988 with "A Nightmare on My Street," which parodied the *A Nightmare on Elm Street* slasher movie franchise, including the film's razor-fingered villain, Freddy Krueger. Later that same year the Fat Boys contributed the song "Are You Ready for Freddy?" featuring Krueger himself, actor Robert Englund, to the *A Nightmare on Elm Street 4: The Dream Master* soundtrack. Big Daddy Kane mentions both Freddy Krueger and Jason Vorhees on early songs. While almost no one seems to want to be overtly associated with horrorcore, several artists have taken credit — from a distance — for conjuring the genre. New York's Big L cited his 1993 single "Devil's Son" as an early horrorcore archetype. Producer Prince Paul says of his group, Gravediggaz, "Gangsta rap had already been so exploited at the time, so we went with horror."

With all of that said, horror-tinged, Gothic rap gets no better than Nicki Minaj's verse on Kanye West's 2010 song "Monster." This seven-minute posse jam also includes West, Jay-Z, Rick Ross, and Bon Iver, but Minaj's sixteen bars overshadow them all. Where West and Jay-Z play "stock characters in a neoliberal white supremacist patriarchal farce," Minaj brings out her characters Roman Zolanski and Harajuku Barbie. In one verse, she adeptly disturbs everything from body normativity to the listener's sensibilities. Minaj raps as both characters, shifting and switching genders and personas all the way through:

> Okay, first things first, I'll eat your brains
> Then I'ma start rocking gold teeth and fangs
> 'Cause that's what a motherfucking monster do
> Hair dresser from Milan, that's the monster 'do
> Monster Giuseppe heel, that's the monster shoe
> Young Money is the roster and a monster crew

The Gothic allows "space for the alterity of the Other," writes Tabish Khair, "the difference *outside* language [...] even when blanked out or registered in negative terms *in* language [...]." In the face of irreconcilable differences, the Gothic allows the monster to be monstrous, the alien to be alien, the ghost to be ghostly. It allows for the possibility of other identities, other worlds, other futures.

### *Twin Infinitives*

On September 7, 1996, Tupac Shakur was shot as he waited at a traffic light in the passenger seat of Suge Knight's car on the Las Vegas strip. He died on September 13. Six months later, on March 9, 1997, Christopher Wallace a.k.a. Biggie Smalls was shot dead in Los Angeles. The two had been embroiled in a media-abetted, bi-coastal battle for hip-hop supremacy, dividing much of the hip-hop nation into two camps: East versus West. Hip-hop is haunted by a number of passed performers. Their ghosts continue to release records, do duets with living acts, and appear on magazine covers. Dead rappers are good business. Patrick Neate writes, "A dead emcee is both fully formed and eminently flexible," and Geoff Harkness adds, "Criminal records sell rap records, but nothing moves product quite like a dead legend." Criminals with permanent records as well as rap records provide more intrigue for fans.

Having found second lives in their sudden deaths, Biggie Smalls and Tupac Shakur are still the two most prominent of these ghosts. They are deities subsequent emcees must pay homage to by mentioning them, performing posthumous duets with them, or aspiring to become them. Justin A. Williams writes, "Rappers who sample martyrs such as Tupac Shakur and Notorious B.I.G. add to the creation of new identities, tributes that often become part of new narratives within the imagined community of hip-hop culture." Williams cites songs by Nas and Jay-Z, who were both contemporaries of Tupac and Biggie. Their collaborations with these dead deities align them with the fallen rappers and their lingering legends.

As I was writing this chapter, young rappers Jimmy Wopo, twenty-one, and XXXtentacion, twenty, were murdered within hours of each other, the former in Pittsburgh and the latter in Deerfield Beach, Florida. Both had hits that much bigger artists had been accused of biting. Kendrick Lamar caught criticism for the similarity of his "Humble" to Wopo's "Elm Street," and Drake's "KMT" was called out for copying the cadence of X's "Look at Me." To be fair, "Elm Street" can be heard as an update to Boogie Down Productions' late-1980s South Bronx anthem "The Bridge is Over," and "Look at Me" wouldn't sound out of place on an early M.O.P. record. Though an infinite regress doesn't excuse plagiarism, it's hard to be a purist when nothing is pure. The songs of the current generation of rappers celebrate violence and oblivion, seemingly tossing away talent and opportunity with reckless carelessness. Like the gangster rappers of generations before them, they prove that there is nothing as cool as youthful nihilism, and nothing quite as deadly. Like Tupac and Biggie who were killed before Wopo and X were even born, their legends will grow in proportion to their absence.

I saw Tupac live only once. In 1990 he was still a member of Oakland's Digital Underground. I caught them opening for Public Enemy in Montgomery, Alabama. At the time, he was serving as Shock G's hype-man and had yet to debut with his verse on their "Same Song" from the 1991 *This is an EP Release*, the follow up to their classic debut, *Sex Packets*. Over the brief next six years, Tupac would become a solo emcee, a hip-hop superstar, and then be shot and killed. That cycle just keeps getting shorter and shorter. Youth might be wasted on the young, but our heroes don't concern themselves with consequences.

### Rock My Hologram

At the end of the music video for his song "99 Problems," Jay-Z is gunned down in the streets of New York City. The song is from his *Black Album* (2003), which was supposed to be his last release. Preparing to retire from the hustle of recording and performing, Jay-Z simulates his own death, imitating the high profile and unsolved slayings of two of his contemporaries, Biggie and Tupac. On the unreleased track, "Most Kings," Jay-Z raps,

> *Hov got flow though he's no Big and Pac, but he's close*
> *How I'm supposed to win? They got me fighting ghosts*

Much as Malcolm X had at the end of his autobiography, Tupac and Biggie anticipated their own deaths in many of their songs. Tupac envisioned his own death in "So Many Tears," "Death Around the Corner," and "Only Fear of Death," among others. In the video for "I Ain't Mad at Cha," he is shot, dies, and sends messages back from heaven. The title of both of Biggie's studio records reference his mortality: 1994's *Ready to Die*, which was the only record released while the young rapper was still alive, and 1997's *Life After Death*, which followed just two weeks after he died.

Tupac Shakur at Coachella, 2012. Photo by Eric Smith-Gunn.

Though they were both posthumously honored with film biographies, Biggie in 2008's *Notorious* and Tupac in 2017's *All Eyez on Me*, Tupac reemerged on stage on April 15, 2012 at the Coachella Music Festival in Indio, California as a "hologram." The ghostly image, which was accompanied on stage by Tupac's peers and former Death Row label mates, Snoop Dogg and Dr. Dre, was actually a nineteenth-century theater special effect known as a Pepper's Ghost, a trick that has also been used to create apparitions in haunted houses. John Henry Pepper, after whom the effect is named, along with Henry Dircks, developed the technique to make ghosts appear on stage during theatrical productions. The effect debuted in December 1862 at the Royal Polytechnic in London and made its way into early film as well. In his book *Gothic Machine*, David J. Jones describes it as, "the spectralization of a live human body: here the magic lantern did not just project slides showing simulacra of the body onto a hidden screen or smoke, but illuminated and cast the eidolon of the body itself onto the stage."

One critic of the time described the effect as "a perfect embodiment of real substance." To which Jones adds, "That 'real substance' is indicative: this was a living, breathing image which seemed to possess, especially post-1863, all the mobility and dimensionality of a three-dimensional body turning in space." Visual effects company Digital Domain used the effect to reanimate Tupac at Coachella, much to the awe of the music fans present and those who have seen it via the internet. Multiple lines are crossed here. This is a new level of resurrecting the past. The use of samples of dead artists reanimates them into new lives. The DJ converges the once separate realms of recorded music and live performance by playing records on turntables as instruments. Tupac's hologram brought his physical body back to life, live on stage.

In the summer of 2015, Chief Keef tried to use a hologram appearance to avoid outstanding warrants in his hometown of Chicago. The young rapper, who became the face of the city's violence once his shirtless video for "I Don't Like" went from South-Side anthem to nationwide hit, moved to the West Coast after signing a multimillion-dollar record deal. At the time of the video, Keef was on house arrest for pointing a gun at a police officer at age fifteen. In 2015 though, he was trying to organize a "Stop the Killing" benefit show for two of his fallen friends. On July 11, thirteen-month-old Dillan Harris was killed by a car fleeing the scene of the shooting that killed fellow rapper Marvin "Capo" Carr.

Originally slated for Pilsen's Redmoon Theatre in Chicago, the show was moved a week later to Craze Fest at Wolf Lake Pavilion in Hammond, Indiana after Chicago's mayor deemed it too dangerous. After saying, "Chicago, we need to stop the violence. Let our kids live," his hologram was able to get through one song before it was shut down. "I know nothing about Chief Keef," the Mayor of Hammond admitted, "All I'd heard was he has a lot of songs about gangs and shooting people — a history that's anti-cop, pro-gang and pro-drug use. He's been basically outlawed in Chicago, and we're not going to let you circumvent Mayor Emanuel by going next door." The mayors of Midwest cities are picking up the cause Tipper Gore's Parents Music Resource Center did in the 1980s: censoring hip-hop by any means necessary. Just as Tupac's hologram reanimated his physical body at Coachella, Keef's was treated the same way his actual presence would have been. Their projections were as effective as their bodies would have been.

### A Ghost is Born

As effective as these illusions might be, no one who sees a hologram or a nineteenth-century version of one thinks they're seeing a real person. These apparitions are illuminated imitations at best. When we hear voices on tape though, something else happens. We don't think of them as disembodied. Rather, we imagine a fictional body that we associate with a real person, living or once living. We hold the ghosts we hear in our heads.

When it comes to capturing the voices of the departed, practitioners and believers of Electronic Voice Phenomena (EVP) take Edison at his word. In a book called *Voices from the Universe*, Friedrich Jürgenson describes leaving a tape recorder out in the Swedish countryside to record bird sounds in the late 1950s. The tape instead picked up messages from both his dead wife and his late mother. Konstantīns Raudive, whose 1971 book, *Breakthrough*, is one of the core texts of EVP, also took Edison at his word, believing that a running tape recorder in a room would pick up voices of ghosts, spirits, and others not of this world. The book includes extensive transcripts of discussions with multiples ghosts both known and unknown to Raudive and his associates. On one, the "experimenter" asks whether the dead are present. A male voice replies, "We are." Of another such tape, Raudive writes of a rather morbid pact:

Sonja L., my friend for many years, died in Riga in 1958 after a long, harrowing illness. We never lost contact and corresponded with each other up to the last days of her life. An agreement had been made between us that the one to die first should give the other a sign of his or her continued existence beyond the grave. Strangely enough I never received the slightest hint from her, either in dreams or in waking consciousness. With her death she seemed to have vanished completely from my life; but in 1965, when I began to experiment with the voice-phenomenon, she manifested her presence on tape.

Of all the quotations from Sonja on that tape, perhaps the most telling is her saying, "Be ready, even without truth."

Just as the Church had a contentious relationship with the Gothic, it also had one with recordings of the alleged voices of dead souls, yet many early EVP experimenters were members of the clergy. "If these be the dead," writes one concerned citizen of the tapes, "and if it indeed be a sin to listen to them, is there any way short of a couple of decades of the Rosary, of inducing them to get to Hell off the air?"

One of Gibson's characters in his 2003 novel *Pattern Recognition* dismisses another's interest in EVP, calling it a case of "apophenia," the finding of meaning in sets of random data. Describing the onset of schizophrenia, the creator of the term called it "delusion as revelation." Apophenia has also been referred to as a "specific experience of an abnormal meaningfulness." These are lovely descriptions of possibly positive hauntings. One could describe the mental labor of listening to a sample-heavy hip-hop track as sort of apophenia. One could describe finding associations in archival records as a sort of apophenia. One could describe connecting disparate areas of subcultural history and aesthetics as a sort of apophenia. One could say that survival in the twenty-first century requires at least a mild case of apophenia. Are they patterns or are they presences?

Ken McLeod writes,

> [T]he recorded voices of Notorious B.I.G. or Tupac heard in posthumous releases already project a sense of an uncanny ephemeral haunting. This disavowal of the embodied body is probably an effect of hegemonic phonographic (and media) history that emphasizes the disembodiment that has accompanied recording and mediation of music performances ever since the late nineteenth century.

From theatre tricks to voices on tapes, we summon the spirits we miss. "In hip-hop, no higher praise can be given to a vocalist than to cut 'n' scratch their voice," writes Harry Allen. "Call it a form of ancestor worship. The scratch is incantatory." Recordings are of the past but are saved for the future. Sampling, whether by scratching a record or searching an archive, reanimates the past into new futures. "We usually think of hauntings as traces from the past," writes Steven Shaviro, "but the future also haunts us with its hints of hope and danger, and its promises or threats of transformation." Whether shimmering on surfaces or hiding in tape hiss, the ghosts are all around us. Our archives are houses haunted by the recordings of dead voices, but when those voices break free, unmoored from the files that bind them, we become their vessels, undead thoughts among the living.

When the head gets hacked, it's the heart that is haunted.

Roots and Wires: Moor Mother Goddess. Photo by Bob Sweeney.

## Chapter Seven

# RETURN TO CINDER

"The matches have been struck, the emotional flames conquered. As the jets move into the aerodynamic triangles and the birds of terrorism fall like babies from a stork to the ground, under the ground where I can be found..."
— Rammellzee, *The Art of Terrorism*

"We will either be saved by the poet or by fire."
— Ernst Jünger, *Aladdin's Problem*

"The moment of real poetry brings all the unsettled debts of history back into play."
— The Situationists International

In 2017's *Blade Runner 2049*, set thirty years after the original film, hologram lovers for hire hover over the streets, and broken holograms of Elvis Presley and Frank Sinatra perform in the remains of a decimated Las Vegas casino. These are not the most forward-thinking uses of virtual presences, considering that outside the movies, legendary emcees are returning from the dead, and younger rappers are skirting the law through the same technologies.

Though these shifts are artificial, thirty years is the widely accepted amount of time it takes for the world to change hands, one generation to another. Now that hip-hop has been around for over thirty years, there's an entire generation that has grown up with it. If you think of technology as the media and devices invented during your lifetime, then the generation here now doesn't think of hip-hop as new media or the contrivances of cyberpunk as new anything. This is just their world now. Where cyberpunk was co-opted and assimilated, its core concerns muted, its conceits mundane, hip-hop embodies and employs its speculative nature. This was not a conscious co-opting but a product of hip-hop's means and methods, of it assimilating its surroundings. One sun may be setting, but the other burns brighter than ever. As Has-Lo puts it, we're "in between P.M. Dawn and Sun Ra."

Changing the world requires creation as much as destruction. Hacking is as much about creating the codes behind things as it is finding and changing them. Steven Shaviro writes,

> These endlessly replicating icons are the very fabric of our lives. That is why appropriation, or sampling, is every-where today: from rap songs, to films and videos, to prose fiction and installation art. Sampling is the best way, and perhaps the *only* way for art to come to terms with a world of brand names, corporate logos, and simulacra.

Turning the dominant codes against themselves, sampling and smuggling meaning across cultural borders are normal modes of art and resistance in the twenty-first century.

Just before starting his 2007 novel, *Spook Country*, William Gibson was invited to a seminar about "illegal facilitators."

He was a member of the Global Business Network, a scenario-planning organization and futures think-tank that has corporate and sometimes government clients. They study these illegal facilitators, which Gibson describes as "crime families that specialize in smuggling across a particular border. They don't care what they're smuggling — if they've got enough money, they'll smuggle whatever it is." The Global Business Network, which disbanded in 2013, emerged from the same group of folks who brought us the Whole Earth Network, the WELL, and other harbingers of early cyberculture.

Futurists studying criminal activity might seem odd, but given our current political divisions and the short-sighted nature of capitalism, criminology is the new sociology. Negotiating borders like the boundary objects between communities of practice or allusions shared by different social groups, illegal facilitators do the same in less legal contexts. Gibson says *Neuromancer* was set around the year 2035 where there's no discernible middle class, nothing between the "posthuman superrich people and the Street, with a capital *S*." In lieu of a middle class, the expanding chasm between the upper and lower classes stretches the social structure and economic disparity far enough to guarantee what criminologists call an *anomic ethics*: those without will do whatever is necessary to provide for themselves with no evident moral dilemmas. When the laws break down, we break the laws.

Hip-hop is a bridge across the breadth between art and commerce, in a bohemia always assimilated by and always assimilating both culture and business. Gibson says:

To the extent that I can still believe in bohemia, which I think is very important to me in some way that I don't yet really understand, to the extent that I still believe in that, I have to believe that there are viable degrees of freedom inherent if not realized in interstitial areas.

The essential tension in hip-hop cultural production, between tradition and innovation, is just such an interstitial area. Taking what's there yet making something new is the current creative impulse. Sampling, stealing, borrowing, disrupting — anything for art and resistance. You can break the law, just don't break the rules.

From the musical samples, lyrical references, recorded memories, and the holographic forms of rapping revenants, the haunting of hip-hop seems endless. If we care at all about authentic experiences, we have to be more mindful of the contexts floating in the media around us. Authenticity comes from the moment we live in, from our experience, not from the objects we buy or their proximity to "the original work." One should resist the longing for an original when none exists. Nostalgia is a weakness, a vulnerability in your network. As RZA says, "We must find and use a logic that's not programmable." Believing counterfeit histories allows us to be hacked by those that would hold us back — remember the implanted memories used in *Blade Runner* to control the Replicants. Of all the things anticipated and invented in the South Bronx so long ago, a crippling nostalgia was not one of them.

## Black Velocities

Cyberpunk might be assimilated, co-opted, and unseen, but its spirit lives on in hip-hop. You can hear it all the way back to Afrika Bambaataa, Grandmaster Flash, and Rammellzee. You can hear it in Tricky, RZA, and Public Enemy. You can hear it in N.W.A., Tupac, and Biggie. You can hear it in Shabazz Palaces, Labtekwon, and Danny Brown; in Juice Aleem, M. Sayyid, and Mike Ladd; You can hear it in dälek, Death Grips, Nicki Minaj, and Moor Mother Goddess; in Antipop Consortium, Cadence Weapon, and Clipping; in Flying Lotus, Jay Electronica, and Open Mike Eagle. You can hear it in the Afrofuturist R&B of Janelle Monáe, Tierra Whack, and Tunde Olaniran. You can hear it in innumerable now and future acts around the world. You can see it in activists, organizations, and conferences like Ingrid LaFleur, the AfroFuturist Affair, Metropolarity, Hip-Hop Chess Federation, the Black Speculative Arts Movement, Afrotech Fest, Afropunk, and Afroflux. You can read it in the theory and criticism of writers like Ytasha L. Womack, Kodwo Eshun, Greg Tate, Dave Tompkins, André Sirois, Christina Sharpe, Su'ad Abdul Khabeer, Simone Brown, André M. Carrington, Adisa Banjoko, Fred Moten, Erik Steinskog, and Tiffany E. Barber; in the speculative fiction of Rasheedah Phillips, Nnedi Okorafor, Nisi Shawl, N. K. Jemisin, Tade Thompson, and Tananarive Due. You can see it in the filmmaking of Boots Riley, Arthur Jafa, Donald Glover, Ava DuVerney, Ryan Coogler, and Jordan Peele. You can find it wherever someone dares to take what's there and make it into something new.

The promised land is a world of words, a possible future

brought into being by making a promise, whether spoken, written, hacked, or coded. "The Earth is layer upon layer of all that has existed, remembered by the dirt," writes adrienne maree brown, "It is time to turn capitalism into a fossil, time to turn the soil, turn the horizon together." When hip-hop started, the Cold War made the end of the world feel inevitable, like it could happen at any moment. It also made it feel likely to come from far away. It loomed like a mushroom cloud in the distance. Now The End feels as intimate as it does imminent. The danger is right nearby, like a knife blade at the ready, likely to come from anywhere. We have certainly outlived a scenario, as Sun Ra once suggested, but the next one is ours. The wrongs of the last one lingering, haunting us like unpaid bills. When music went from performed to recorded to performed using recordings, there was a break, a break with time as it had been conceived up until then.

"We wield 'science fiction' voice and word to manifest world-paradigms necessary for our survival," write the activists behind Philadelphia's Metropolarity project:

*Our neighborhoods, our networks*
*The whole spirit of the city*
*Was already sci-fi*

*And we were tired of the bullshit*
*Calling itself sci-fi*
*Meaning the anti-Black colonizer man's fantasy of empire*
*Which would have us die off and be forgotten*
*In the ongoing campaign to erase how we all got here.*

Sun Ra once said that he was attracted to the impossible because everything possible had been done, and the world hadn't changed. "Perhaps the most egregious thing we are taught," adds brown, "is that we should just be really good at what's already possible, to leave the impossible alone." Who's deciding what's possible for us? Who's drawing these lines? We need to stop asking for permission or forgiveness. We need to be trying the impossible with impunity.

For example, the internet promised us diversity but has given us division instead. Minister of Crossroads and founding member of Metropolarity, M. Eighteen Téllez writes, "We're the ghost of 1990s internet come back to remind you what it was like to live adventurously without the trappings of your pre-signified body." We need to put the *punk* back into cyberculture, to make our numbers known again, to make ourselves dangerous again. "You have to forge yourself into a weapon," Téllez says.

We need to unite and become hackers ourselves now more than ever. The original Hacker Ethic isn't enough. We don't need to just make room, we need to change the defaults. We need more of those nameless nerds, nodes in undulating networks of cyber-disobedience. Hackers of all kinds need to appear, swarm, attack, and then disappear again into the dark fiber of the deep web. To unhide the hidden transcripts, restore the deleted scenes. To move these desires from latent to blatant. To subvert the accepted narratives. To sample, manipulate, and remix the stories we're given. To tell our own as loud as we can. To make manifest the change we know is possible.

We're not passing the torch, we're torching the past.

# FURTHER LISTENING

While again I would argue, as I have for many pages, that all hip-hop is futuristic, here is an incomplete but annotated list of some that is consciously both forward-looking and future-sounding.

Afrika Bambaataa and the Soulsonic Force, "Planet Rock" (1982): This "space ship landing in the ghetto" is one of the early glimpses of black cyberpunk.

Airborn Audio, *Good Fortune* (2004): During an Antipop Consortium hiatus, members M. Sayyid and High Priest continued their journey into the future with Airborn Audio. Essential.

Antipop Consortium: One of the most forward-sounding acts in hip-hop, APC's entire catalog sounds like it's from the far-flung future. Start with *Arrhythmia* (Warp, 2002) and then try *Florescent Black* (Big Dada, 2009). See also: Airborne Audio, Beans, M. Sayyid.

Babbletron, *Mechanical Royalty* (Embedded, 2003): Perhaps best known for launching the brief rap career of emcee Cool Calm Pete, *Mechanical Royalty* is that rare hip-hop concept that works. Babbletron bend space, time, science, and the cosmos into classic boom-bap for the new millennium, smuggling moon rocks and a "Space Tech Banana Clip" for the deep-space 9mm.

Beans: The most active of Antipop Consortium's separate ways, Beans' entire catalog is from a time we haven't gotten to yet.

Cadence Weapon: From the arcade funk of "Sharks" to his *TRON Legacy* mixtape, Cadence Weapon is always a few clicks ahead of the times.

Cannibal Ox, *The Cold Vein* (Def Jux, 2001): As soon as you hear the opening tones of "Iron Galaxy," you know you're on another planet.

Clipping: Clipping bring together the noise of the streets with the storytelling of the stage. Their three members include a soundtrack composer, a performance studies Ph.D., and a member of the *Hamilton* cast. *Splendor & Misery* (Sub Pop, 2016) and the follow-up single "The Deep" were both nominated for Hugo awards.

Cybotron, *Clear* (Fantasy, 1990): An updated reissue of their 1983 debut *Enter*, *Clear* is some sort of cosmic electro-pop-funk blend, complete with mechanized rhythms and robot voices. You'll wonder why it wasn't sampled to death upon its original release.

dälek: I think my first attempt at describing dälek's sound involved something about a cross between Public Enemy and My Bloody Valentine. They're so much more than that. Their records are a mix of angry and intricate lyrics, booming beats, dreamy feedback drones, and nightmare non-notes, all perfect examples of how unique and powerful hip-hop can be. By turns noisy, militant, and majestic, dälek stay pushing ahead with unwavering purpose.

Danny Brown, *Atrocity Exhibition* (2017): Drug use is an aspect of cyberpunk that I barely mention in this book, but Danny Brown has it covered. Well worthy of both its nominal forebears, *Atrocity Exhibition* is rap at its artistic peak.

Death Grips: The Trickster fog gets no thicker than Death Grips. When they're not duping the industry one way or another, they make some of the noisiest hip-hop out.

Deltron 3030, *Deltron 3030* (45 Ark, 2000): Dan the Automator, Del the Funky Homosapien, and Kid Koala's rap-concept record, *Deltron 3030*, might be the most obvious example of futuristic hip-hop. As Del says, "Upgrade your grey matter 'cause one day it may matter." See also: Dr. Octagon.

Digable Planets, *Reachin' (A New Refutation of Time and Space)* (Pendulum, 1993); *Blowout Comb* (Pendulum, 1994): Their debut inadvertently became a jazz-rap classic and its follow up is an overlooked essential. See also: Shabazz Palaces.

Divine Styler: Divine Styler has been not-so-quietly building an alternate hip-hop reality, from 1989's *Word Power* (Rhyme $yndicate) to 1998's *Wordpower, Vol. 2: Directrix* (DTX) and on to 2014's *Def Mask* (Gamma Performa).

DJ Qbert, *Extraterrestria* (Thud Rumble, 2014); *GalaXXXian* (Thud Rumble, 2014): One of the best turntablists on the planet has stated that he often thinks of scratching as communication in alien tongues. Here he put together a double set of concepts on these two records: one from outer-space, and one from right here on Earth.

DJ Spooky, *Songs of a Dead Dreamer* (Asphodel, 1996); *Drums of Death* (with Dave Lombardo; Thirsty Ear, 2005): The latter of these features not only Slayer's ex-drummer but also Chuck D reworking a few classic Public Enemy songs.

Dr. Octagon, *Dr. Octagonecologyst* (DreamWorks, 1996): Pornographic gothic-horror science-fiction rap? Yes! Kool Keith as Dr. Octagon covers it all, and with production by Dan the Automator and scratches by DJ Qbert, the music matches the lyricism. See also: Deltron 3030, Ultramegnetic MCs.

Dream Warriors, *And Now the Legacy Begins* (1990): Set off by the minor hit "My Definition of a Boombastic Jazz Style," Toronto's Dream Warriors' debut also sports speculative songs like "Tune from the Missing Channel" and "Voyage Through the Multiverse."

Egyptian Lover, *On the Nile* (1984): Backward to go forward, Egyptian Lover's 1984 electro-chant "Egypt, Egypt" was a B-boy staple. It still sounds like it's from decade hence instead of decades passed.

El-P, *Fantastic Damage* (Def Jux, 2002); *I'll Sleep When You're Dead* (Def Jux, 2007): Dropping within months of 9/11, *Fantastic Damage* is the sound of the city crumbling with spaced-out gangster shit like "Deep Space 9mm," "DeLorean," "Stepfather Factory," "Constellation Funk," and the title track. *I'll Sleep When You're Dead* opens with a David Lynch sample and features the Mars Volta and Trent Reznor, among others. See also: Run the Jewels, Company Flow.

Freestyle, *Freestyle* (Pandisc, 1990): The robotic dance grooves of Freestyle still sound like they're being beamed down from the stars.

Grandmaster Flash, "The Adventures of Grandmaster Flash on the Wheels of Steel" (Sugar Hill, 1981): Still the ruler by which beat-driven, sample-based music is measured.

Ho99o9, *United States of Horror* (Toys Have Powers, 2017):
Ho99o9 bring the sonic terrors not only from the worst
dystopian futures imaginable but also the illest genres:
power electronics, goth, punk, hardcore, and horrorcore
hip-hop. If it's dark and dangerous, it's here. Play loud.

JPEGMAFIA, *Veteran* (Deathbomb Arc, 2018): As glitchy as
he is gangster, JPEGMAFIA is an actual veteran of the
armed forces. This sounds more like he's a veteran of
making music from after the apocalypse.

Juice Aleem: Since New Flesh split up, Juice Aleem has
kept at it, steady pushing ahead with records, writings,
conferences, and other forward-thinking activities and
events. See also: New Flesh for Old.

Labtekwon: Baltimore emcee Labtekwon was described
by Chuck D as "the Thelonius Monk of hip-hop" and
by *Afro Punk* as a cross between Jean-Michel Basquiat
and Nikola Tesla. He's an anthropologist, a professor, a
writer, an emcee, and a skateboarder. His first record
came out over two decades ago.

M. Sayyid, *Error Tape 1* (self-released, 2017): M. Sayyid
is Antipop Consortium's resident storyteller with an
unmistakable Slick-Rick-from-the-Dark-Side vibe. Just
listen to "9.99" from their *Tragic Epilogue* (75 Ark, 2000)
or "Z St." from *Arrhythmia* (Warp, 2002). From "Eon" to
"Silver Light" to "Beams from Infinity," *Error Tape 1* is
all interstellar intricacies. See also: Antipop Consortium,
Airborn Audio.

Mantronix: With their electro-beats, frenetic scratching,
and robot voices, Mantronix is another old-school
group that still sounds like they're from the future.
Just listen to "Needle to the Groove" from *The Album*

(Sleeping Bag, 1985) or "Who is It?" from *Music Madness* (Sleeping Bag, 1986).

Mike Ladd *Welcome to the Afterfuture* (Ozone, 2000): While all of Mike Ladd's music is progressive and futuristic, *Welcome to the Afterfuture* is his most self-consciously science fictional. It includes songs like "Planet 10," "To the Moon's Contractor," "Red Eye to Jupiter," "Bladerunners" (featuring Company Flow), the title track, and of course, "5,000 Miles West of the Future."

Moor Mother: As a part of Philadelphia's Afro-Futurist Affair, Moor Mother Goddess has been creating soundtracks to their time-traveling alternate futures for years. On her own work, she rages against wrongs of all kinds. It's a righteous, beautiful noise. Go get *Fetish Bones* (Don Giovanni, 2016).

N.W.A., *Straight Outta Compton* (Ruthless, 1988): The first three songs on *Straight Outta Compton* are battle cries for the future of an ignored population. They ushered in an era that has yet to end. As Ben Westhoff writes in his book, *Original Gangstas*, "Gangsta rap, more than any other art form, made black life a permanent part of the American conversation." This record had more to do with that than any other.

New Flesh for Old, *Equilibrium* (Big Dada, 1999); *Understanding* (Big Dada, 2002); *Universally Dirty* (Big Dada, 2006): Overlooked and underrated, New Flesh was a blend of many styles from all over that added up to the future. See also: Juice Aleem.

New Kingdom, *Heavy Load* (Gee Street, 1993); *Paradise Don't Come Cheap* (Gee Street, 1996): New Kingdom's sloppy, bluesy funk might not sound futuristic at first listen, but it is definitely not of this time — or of this world, as the "Came to Earth on a rocketship!" sample at the beginning of "Co-Pilot" suggests.

Pharoahe Monch, *W.A.R. (We Are Renegades)* (Duck Down, 2011); *PTSD: Post Traumatic Stress Disorder* (W.A.R. Media, 2014): These two records find the veteran New York emcee telling sort of a hip-hop *2112* story about independence struggling against the establishment.

Playboi Carti: Though he gets lumped in with "mumble rap" artists, Playboi Carti is much more sophisticated than that crowd. He makes music defiant to the sounds of the time in general and to its own genre specifically. There's nothing more cyberpunk than that.

Prefuse 73: Scott Herren's glitchy hip-hop productions sound cobbled together out of leftover hip-hop tracks from some future South Bronx.

Public Enemy, *It Takes a Nation of Millions to Hold Us Back* (Def Jam, 1988); *Fear of a Black Planet* (Def Jam, 1990): These might be the two most important records on this list. They define the future like no others before or since.

Rammellzee vs K-Rob, "Beat Bop" 12" (Profile, 1983): "Produced" by Jean-Michel Basquiat, "Beat Bop" introduced the world to the Rammellzee and his "Gangsta Duck" voice. Classic material. See also: *This is What You Made Me* (2003); *Bi-Conicals of the Rammellzee* (Gomma, 2004).

RZA, *Bobby Digital in Stereo* (Gee Street, 1998); *Ghost Dog: The Way of the Samurai* (Epic, 1999); *Afro Samurai: The Album* (Koch, 2007): RZA's Bobby Digital persona is a little wilder than RZA usually is, a little more raw. His soundtrack work is a world unto itself. See also: Wu-Tang Clan, Gravediggaz.

Shabazz Palaces, *Lese Majesty* (Sub Pop, 2014); *Quazarz: Born on a Gangster Star* (Sub Pop, 2017); *Quazarz vs. The Jealous Machines* (Sub Pop, 2017): From the opening tones of "Dawn in Luxor" off *Lese Majesty*, you know you're off to somewhere else. The latter two are conceptual companions, and they're all interstellar trips worth taking.

Sun Ra: Sun Ra recorded and released more records than any other artist in the twentieth century, so advice as to an entry point varies. Try *Jazz in Silhouette* (El Saturn, 1959), *Lanquidity* (Philly Jazz, 1978), and of course, *Space is the Place* (Blue Thumb, 1973).

Techno Animal, *The Brotherhood of the Bomb* (2001): On their last record, the industrial duo of Justin K. Broadrick (of Godflesh, Jesu, etc.) and Kevin Martin (of GOD, Ice, etc.) brought along guests like dälek, Rob Sonic, Antipop Consortium, El-P, and Toastie Taylor of New Flesh for Old.

Tricky, *Maxinquaye* (4th & B'Way, 1995); *Nearly God* (Island, 1996); *Pre-Millennium Tension* (Island, 1996); *Ununiform* (False Idols, 2017): Tricky's first three records seemed to launch a whole new form. It was dubbed "trip-hop," but its darkness always made me think of it as goth-hop. Whatever you call it, his latest, *Ununiform*, could be called a return to the form he started.

Tunde Olaniran, *Transgressor* (Quite Scientific, 2015): Tunde Olaniran's spaced-out soul is from some future Flint, Michigan where pop music is fun and funky above all else. Just have a quick listen to "Namesake," "Diamonds," or the title track.

Ultramagnetic MCs, *Critical Beatdown* (Next Plateau, 1988): Where other producers were looping and extending breaks, Ced-Gee was one of the first to chop and sequence samples. Couple that with the racy, spacey lyrics of him and Kool Keith, and you've got something not of this time or world. Hank Shocklee of the Bomb Squad has cited the record as an influence on Public Enemy's *It Takes a Nation of Millions to Hold Us Back* (Def Jam, 1988).

Wu-Tang Clan: Another crew that manages to sound traditional and fresh at the same time, their sprawling number is matched by their lyrical styles and skills. Just listen to Inspectah Deck's verse on "Triumph" from *Wu-Tang Forever* (Loud, 1998) or Method Man's verse on "Campfire" from *8 Diagrams* (SRC/Universal Motown, 2007) or anything from *Enter the Wu-Tang (36 Chambers)* (Loud, 1993). See also: Their numerous solo records.

The X-Ecutioners: Along with the Invizibl Skratch Piklz, the X-Men expanded cutting-and-scratching turntablism into live improvised jam sessions. Their original line-up, including Rob Swift, Total Eclipse, Mista Sinista, and Roc Raida, went from DJ battles to a full-on assault on pop culture with Billboard-charting full-length records, collaborations with Linkin Park and Mike Patton, and a Gap commercial. See also: DJ QBert.

X Clan, *To the East, Blackwards* (4th & B'Way, 1990); *Xodus* (Polydor, 1992): Like many others on this list but perhaps most deliberately, the X Clan's futuristic funk also went backwards to go forward. Van glorious!

# NOTES

*Preface*

11 "Space, that endless...": Young, 2012, p. 298.

11 "Let us imagine...": Rose, 1994, p. 39.

13 Where *Criminal Minded* is: Admittedly, KRS-One did run P.M. Dawn off the stage years after Scott La Rock passed. So, the Blastmaster wasn't completely dedicated to peace thereafter; See Matos, 2011.

14 Long before hip-hop went: As Maher puts it, "there wouldn't be a rap music industry if it weren't for mixtapes [...] the development of hip-hop revolves around [them as] a singularly crucial but often overlooked medium"; 2005, p. 138; See also Ball, 2011; Kugelberg, 2015; Oworko, 2011.

14 A lot of people: See Alim, 2006; Alim, Ibrahim, and Pennycock, 2009; Clayton, 2016; Fernandes, 2011; Neate, 2003.

14 Though their roots: See for example, Cobb, 2007, p. 7.

15 "I didn't see a subculture...": Quoted in *Ego Trip*, 2012.

15 "Hip-hop didn't invent...": Quoted in Toogood, 2012.

## *Chapter One: Endangered Theses*

17 "The only important elements...": Delany, 1966, p. 70; Oscar a.k.a. The Lump, the main character Comet Jo's sidekick, is an artificial lifeform. "Lump" is short for Linguistic Ubiquitous Multi-Plex. The Lump's use of the name Oscar is an allusion to Oscar Wilde.

17 "Tricky's *Maxinquaye* is a kind...": Mudede, 2010.

18 Tricky and his muse: Batey, 2010.

18 The music world: I stole "wild at heart and weird on top" from David Lynch and Barry Gifford's *Wild at Heart*; See Lynch & Gifford, 1990; Gifford, 1990.

18 According to accounts: Ali, 1996.

18 "the lost Motherland": Reynolds, 2013, p. 333.

18 "I found out later...": Quoted in Reynolds, 2000.

18 "double consciousness": Du Bois, 1903, passim.

19 "It has become increasingly...": Fisher, 2014, p. 50.

19 "Any old stupor...": Reynolds, 2013, p. 330.

19 "Fragments of Trevor Horn...": Mudede, 2010.

20 "Diasporic intimacy is haunted...": Boym writes, "Diasporic intimacy can be approached only through indirection and intimation, through stories and secrets. It is spoken in a foreign language that reveals the inadequacies of translation. Diasporic intimacy is not opposed to uprootedness and defamiliarization but is constituted by it. Diasporic intimacy does not promise an unmediated emotional fusion, but only a precarious affection — no less deep, yet aware of its transience"; 2001, p. 252.

20 It's that feeling when: I lifted this expression from Tracy Morgan (see Morgan, 2009, p. xv), and he's interpolating Rakim's lyrics from "I Know You Got Soul" (1987), which states, "It ain't where you're from, it's where you're at."

20 *False Media*: Public Enemy, "Don't Believe the Hype," 1988; The Roots, "False Media," 2006.

20 Scholars, researchers, and journalists: For a woefully inept analysis of the rise of rap music, see Everett M. Rogers' *Diffusion of Innovations*. Where Rogers has set the standard for the study of the spread innovation with his diffusion theory, his generalizations about rap music and hip-hop culture are telling look at how many established scholars have failed in their addressing of the topic; Rogers, 2003, pp. 220-221; For further discussion, see also McLeod, 2002; Petchauer, 2012, pp. 2-5; Wang, 2006.

22 "[…] music so postindustrial": Adler, 1990, p. 56.

22 "It was so off-base…": Adler, 1999, p. 145.

This attitude persists: Just a few years later, the November 29, 1993 issue of *Newsweek* featured a Snoop Dogg cover story called "When is Rap 2 Violent?" And so it has gone; See Westhoff, 2016, p. 251.

23 Keef is a known: See Harkness, 2014, p. 1-2.

23 A few months later: Harkness, 2014, p. 192.

25 "Mr. West has rarely…": Caramanica, 2012.

25 "There probably ought to…": Brown, 2012, p. 5.

26 "THE defining document…": Caramanica, 2012.

26 "I think it's pretty likely…": Quoted in Conner, 2012.

26 One of the core arguments: For a thorough and astute argument for hip-hop's being inherently futuristic, see Galli, 2009.

26 Technologically enabled cutting: McLeod & DiCola, 2011; Sirois, 2016.

27 In African-American traditions: Gates, 1988, passim.

27 "Brand new, you're retro.": Tricky, 1995.

### Chapter Two: Margin Prophets

29 "We are the hackers...": Wark, 2004, p. 1.

29 "So what is punk?...": Porush, 1992, p. 256.

29 "You'll never represent...": Tricky, "Brand New You're Retro," 1995.

30 "Armageddon has been in...": Public Enemy, 1988.

30 "I came to understand...": Email correspondence with Mark Dery July 6, 2017; In this same exchange, Dery goes on to describe Grandmaster Flash and the Furious Five's 1982 single "The Message" as "politically radical avant-garde pop music, made by survivors of a racist econopocalypse amid the ruins of that alien planet, '70s New York."

30 With its burnt-out: See George, 2002; Fernandez, 2007; Kelly, 1985.

31 "In the cyberpunk future...": Anderson, 2014.

31 Most of the O.G. cyberpunks: Evans, 2012; As Istvan Csicsery-Ronay, Jr. writes, "What are we to make of a style whose supposed practitioners consistently distance themselves from the term? Cyberpunk often seems to live mainly in commentary about some absent text, a Borgesian or Lemian gloss constructing its own foundation from the roof downward."; 1992, p. 26.

31 "like the original punks...": Anderson, 2014.

31 *Atomic Punk*: Van Halen, 1978.

31 For our purposes: As Arthur Miller once said, "An era can be said to end when its basic illusions have been exhausted."; Quoted in Booker, 2014, p. 1519.

31 "The Message": Nelson George (1994) describes "The Message" as "one of the greatest raps, whose ominous synthesizer arrangement accentuates its images of apocalyptic chaos..."; 1994, p. 76.

31 Mike Ladd's welcoming us: Mike Ladd released a record in 2000 called *Welcome to the Afterfuture* (Ozone Music).

32 By 1999, *not* having: In 1999 Gateway Computers ran a print advertisement that read, "Okay, who doesn't have a computer yet?"

32 "I started hearing about...": Rucker, 2011, p. 202.

32 It was in that year that: Bruce Bethke's "Cyberpunk" story was first published in *Amazing Science Fiction Stories* in November of 1983.

32 "We started writing cyberpunk...": Quoted in Evans, 2012.

33 "Cyberpunk was identified as..." Interview with Pat Cadigan, April 29, 2018.

33 In addition to those mentioned: For more on the originals of Cyberpunk and its core concerns, see Anderson, 2016; Blake, 2013; Butler, 2000; Cavallaro, 2000; Heuser, 2003; Kelly & Kessel, 2007; McCaffery, 1991; Slusser & Shippey, 1992; and, of course, Sterling, 1986; Sterling has also designated a style he calls "slipstream," writing, "Slipstream tends, not to 'create' new worlds, but to *quote* them, chop them up out of context, and turn them against themselves"; See Sterling, 1989, p. 77.

34 While it sometimes seems: See Sterling, 1986.

34 "cyber-Gothic": Punter, 1996, p. 173.

34 These aren't predictions: Singer and lyricist Robert Calvert describes the band Hawkwind's science-fiction inspired music: "It's not predicting what is going to happen, it's the mythology of the Space Age, in the way that rocketships and interplanetary travel parallel with the heroic voyages of earlier times."; Quoted in Heller, 2018, p. 48; Others have described science fiction as defining the times in which it was written as opposed to predicting the future: Frederic Jameson, et al.

34 Any web wanderer: Gibson came up with the term "cyberspace" in 1981. It first appeared in his story "Burning Chrome" in the July, 1982 issue of *Omni Magazine*.; See Gibson, 2012, p. 193.

34 So strong was the word: Woolley, 1992.

35 "the unpaid Bill": Henthorne, 2011, p. 39.

35 "Everyone is going to...": Quoted in Jones, 2011.

35 "an increasingly science fictional...": Quoted in Eshun, 1996.

35 "Clarke was spending all...": Quoted in Miller, 2007, p. 344.

35 "When I started writing...": Quoted in Van Bakel, 1995; As Vernon Reid tells Greg Tate, "Steely Dan is the ultimate jaded-hipster/post-beatnik clique whose songs are an oblique catalog of obsessions, twisted lives, the pleasures and dangers of underground economics. They probably have the most hit songs devoted to a life of crime outside of hip-hop in pop. They also chronicle a kind of noirish disillusionment with the romance of the American ideal: like Bogart playing Philip Marlowe, or Otis 'Sitting on the Dock of the Bay'; forever brokenhearted and forever haunted. Their song 'Any Major Dude' is about a more

experienced hustler having the compassion to share the dark knowledge ant hustler would."; Quoted in Tate, 2003, p. 110; Steely Dan also owed homage to science fiction; See Heller, 2017, pp. 136-137.

36 Knowing the character: As Dery puts it, "A collective pop unconscious is presumed; the text is intended to be read *through* the accreted meanings of its intertextual references"; 1996, p. 92, italics in original.

36 "We don't quite live...": Quoted in Evans, 2012.

37 "Small-scale technologies...": Turner, 2006, p. 240.

37 "Computers are to the...": Rucker, 1988, p. 23. This quotation has also been attributed to Dr. Timothy Leary; See Sterling, 1986, p. xi.

37 Gibson tuned in and: Scott Bukatman describes the link between the counterculture of the 1960s and the computer culture of the 1980s as "central to understanding cyberpunk"; See Bukatman, 1993, pp. 139-140.

37 "Patient Zero of what...": Gibson, 2002.

37 Mind-altering drugs: See Neale, 2000.

37 "I think bohemians are...": Quoted in Van Bakel, 1995.

37 I like to think: Greg Tate calls it a "maroon space"; See Russonello, 2015.

37 "The story of this decade...": Fisher, 2009.

38 Gibson cites punk: Gibson says, "Punk was the last viable bohemia that we've seen, perhaps the last bohemian movement of all time. I'm afraid that bohemians will eventually come to be seen as a byproduct of the industrial civilization; and if we're in fact at the end of industrial civilization, there may be no more bohemians. That's scary. It's possible that commercialization has

become so sophisticated that it's no longer possible to do that bohemian thing."; See Van Bakel, 1995.

38 Perhaps this says: Gibson says, "Look what they did to those poor kids in Seattle! It took our culture literally three weeks to go from a bunch of kids playing in a basement club to the thing that's on the Paris runways. At least, with punk, it took a year and a half. And I'm sad to see the phenomenon disappear."; See Eshun, 1996.

38 *Ride the Fader*: Chavez, 1996. Shout out to Clay Tarver.

38 Computer hackers represent: Katie Hafner and John Markoff open their 1991 book, *Cyberpunk: Outlaws and Hackers on the Computer Frontier*, writing, "We set out to investigate a computer underground that is the real-life version of cyberpunk, science fiction that blends high technology with outlaw culture"; p. 9; Chude-Sokei writes of cyberpunk, "As a genre or movement, it is known for its fascination with reinvention and the use of technology in ways opposed to its original intentions by communities unexpected to have access to those technologies, from Japan to Brazil to Arica."; 2016, p. 154. See also Mungo & Clough, 1992, p. 201.

38 In the broader view: Renowned hacker Kevin Mitnick writes, "The thrill and satisfaction of doing things I wasn't supposed to do were just too great. I was consumed by a fascination with the technology of phones and computers. I felt like an explorer, traveling cyberspace without limitations, sneaking into systems for the pure thrill and satisfaction, outsmarting engineers with years of experience, figuring out how to bypass security obstacles, learning how things worked"; 2011, p. 28.

39 Like the African Diaspora: Krims, 2000; Potter, 1995; Rose, 1994.

39 Hip-hop music is a patchwork: Gates, 2010; Lazerine & Lazerine, 2008; Potter, 1995.

40 "Scratch music, whose...": Sterling, 1986, p. xii.

40 These DJs are just: Several scholars make this argument, including Sam Delany, Ken Mcleod, and Nabeel Zuberi. Zuberi writes, "The machinations of hip-hop work belong to a continuum of black 'misuses' of technology from the broken bottleneck applied to the blues guitar, and the oil drum bashed and buffed to create Trinidad steel sound, to the Roland 808 drum machine [...] [an instrument] dumped by many musicians, and [...] picked up secondhand by black producers in Chicago who turned its 'unmusical' sounds into the basis of house music"; 2001, p. 149.

40 "hip-hop culture retrofits...": Dery, 1994, p. 185. See also Gilroy, 2010; Steinskog, 2018, p. 181; Tate, 2003; Weheliye, 2005.

40 *A Saucerful of Secrets*: Pink Floyd, 1968.

40 Driven to stand out: Ogg, 1999, p. 26-27.

40 "I couldn't afford...": Quoted in George, 2004, p. 49.

41 "peek-a-boo": Fricke & Ahearne, 2002, p. 59.

41 He also perfected: Wallmark, 2009, pp. 531-532.

42 "I was sure everybody...": Flash, 2008, p. 82-83.

42 "*And nobody got it!*": Flash, 2008, p. 83; Italics in original.

42 "I was just watching him...": Quoted in Flash, 2008, p. 83.

42 Though Dr. Dre cites: Westhoff, 2016.

42 "My first exposure…": Quoted in, Fernando, 1994, p. 237-238. It should also be noted that Dre's first group, The World Class Wreckin' Cru, had a song called "Planet" that evolved pretty directly from Bambaataa's "Planet Rock"; see Westhoff, 2016, p. 27.

42 "To understand the…": CK Smart, p. 75. Nelson George writes that Flash's "Adventures…" "captures the spirit and creativity of the city's summertime block parties better than any record I've ever heard"; 1992, p. 73.

43 "Hip-hop humanizes…": Allen, 2000, p. 91.

43 Kool Herc started: Bradley & Dubois, 2010; Chang, 2005; Fricke & Ahearn, 2002; Rose, 1994.

43 "From my perspective…": Sirois, 2016, p. XVII.

44 "From what I have seen…" Sirois, 2016, p. 78.

44 "dialectic between hip-hop DJs…": Sirois, 2016, p. 120.

### Chapter Three: Fruit of the Loot

47 "This confusion and…": Chambers, 1986, p. 193-194.

47 "For a fragment of…": Benjamin, 1999, p. 470.

47 "The White man will…": Reed, 1972, p. 194.

48 As the surveillance: For further depth on computer hacker history from MIT in the 1960s to phone phreaking to WikiLeaks and Anonymous, see Coleman, 2015; Greenberg, 2012; Levy, 1984; Mungo & Clough, 1992; Olson, 2012; Slatalla & Quittner, 1995; Sterling, 1992.

48 "It is the End of…": Sterling, 1992, p. 301.

48 The Hacker Ethic states: Levy, 1984, p. 40.

48 Tactical media, so-called: Geert Lovink writes, "Tactical

networks are all about an imaginary exchange of concepts outbidding and overlaying each other. Necessary illusions. What circulates are models and rumors, arguments and experiences of how to organize cultural and political activities, get projects financed, infrastructure up and running and create informal networks of trust which make living in Babylon bearable"; 2002, p. 254; See also Branwyn, 1994; Lievrouw, 2011; Raley, 2009.

49 "See what I have made...": Raley, 2009, p. 2; Italics in original.

49 Wires may be wormholes: Stephenson, 1996.

49 At the end of the 1980s: As Daniel Lanois writes, in the late 1970s: "[...] the term sample had not been invented yet — I called them traps. I would catch little fragments from vinyl records and then manipulate my sources to the point of nonrecognition"; 2010, p. 22.

49 The Turtles sued: McLeod, 2005.

49 In another case of: McLeod, 2005; Hess, 2007.

50 In hip-hop, samples: Brewster & Broughton, 2006; Katz, 2004; 2012.

50 "Using everything from...": Interview with Juice Aleem, July 23, 2018.

50 Four record labels sued: McLeod, 2005.

50 Both are a part of: Braidotti, 2013.

51 "information-processing systems...": Hayles, 1999, p. 113.

51 "montage of loosely...": McLuhan, 1962, p. xxix.

52 "his hands like...": Flash, 2008, p. 88.

52 "A 68-year-old woman...": Weingarten, 2010, p. 37.

52 Conceived as a combination: Fernando, Jr., 1994, p. 137.

52 Where their 1987 debut: Myrie, 2008, p.60.

53 "it sounded like…": Quoted in McLeod, 2005, p. 66.

53 It remains one of: See Hinds, 2002; Myrie, 2008; Weingarten, 2010; et al.

54 "Black punk rock": Quoted in Ogg, p. 79.

54 "We're media hijackers": Quoted in Ogg, p. 80.

54 "We got sued religiously…": Quoted in Brian Coleman, 2005, p. 176-177. Harry Allen says of the song, "It's really speaking to the way the industry handles technological change."; quoted in McLeod, 2005, p. 66.

54 "Found this mineral…": Public Enemy, 1988.

54 "Cultural memory is most…": Hirsch & Smith, 2002, p. 7.

54 "witness effect": Nichols & Moon, 1992, p. 103; 1994, p. 47-48.

55 "against a power structure…": Eshun, 2003, p. 289.

55 "Afrofuturism approaches contemporary…": Eshun, 2003, p. 299.

55 An intertextual view: Fairclough, 1992.

55 "when a thing…": Quoted in Gleick, 2008.

55 Though a dialog between: Eshun, 2003; Donna Haraway states that "the boundary between science fiction and social reality is an optical illusion."; Haraway, 1991, p. 194.

55 Of all forms of art: Patke, 2005.

55 Once recordings become: Patke, 2005.

56 Mechanical reproduction, though: Benjamin, 1968.

56 "I think one important…": Eshun & Sagar, 2007, p. 131.

56 The selection of particular: Weick & Roberts, 1993; As Daniel Lanois puts it, "*Remembering* is just another word for choosing."; 2010, p. 13.

56 The past matters here: Jacques Derrida called our

obsession with recording "archive fever," writing, "The archivization *produces* as much as it *records* the event"; Derrida, 1996, p. 16-17; my emphasis.

56 The turntable is a: Wershier-Henry, 1995, p. 246

57 Grandmaster DXT: Peters writes, "The phonograph, as the name suggests, is a means of writing."; 1999, p. 160; Chambers calls memory "the skin stretched over the world across which desire, emotions, and expressions flow. Memory evokes the eroticisation of the past." He goes on to say that memory is "sustained and guarded by language, in the record of images, words, and sounds," and "Not only do we recall our past in music, but the very techniques that permit us to return there, recordings, are a form of inscription, of writing."; 1997, p. 234; Some have gone so far as to call the brain a "conscious phonograph"; See Draaisma, 2000, pp. 85-93; See also Gilroy, 1985; Wershier-Henry, 1995, p. 246.

57 We use the past: As Patrick Greaney writes, "Quotation evokes those possibilities. By repeating the past, artists and writers may be attempting to repeat that past's unrealized futures"; 2014, p. x.

57 Unlike the oral: Ricoeur, 2004.

57 To quote from records: As Stewart Ewen puts it, "Ripped from its original context, its original meanings are lost"; Ewen, 1984, p. 93. See also Benjamin, 1968; Schwartz, 1996; McGlone, 2005a; 2005b.

57 When the archives move: Ernst, 2013; Smith, 1998.

57 "I just changed the chorus...": Quoted in McLeod & DiCola, 2011, p. 32.

57 "That sound is not only...": Quoted in Chart Attack, 2006.

58 he added the block-rocking: See Bradley, 2010, p. 16;

Howard, 2004, p. 267.

58 "The sound of 'Planet Rock': Quoted in Bascunan, 2016; George also described Bambaataa's sound as "space-rap."; 1992, p. 55; Bambaataa himself says that with "Planet Rock," "we was really trying to reach the Black, Latino, and the punk rock whites."; Quoted in Fricke & Ahearn, 2002, p. 315; Jeff Chang describes Bambaataa as an "original gangster, post-civil rights peacemaker, Black riot rocker, breakbeat archaeologist, interplanetary mystic, conspiracy theorist, Afrofuturist, hip-hop activist, twenty-first-century griot"; Chang 2005, p. 92.

58 The pair put together: Flür, 2000, p. 247.

58 In another example: See Blistein, 2016; *BBC News*, 2016.

59 "[…] such uses of other artists'…": Flür, 2000, p. 249.

59 Philosopher of science: Kuhn, 1977.

59 "What separates 'biting'…": Bradley, 2008, p. 150; my italics.

59 Many still see sampling: See, for example, Dettmar & Richey,1999, pp. 1-15.

59 "To my ears…": Flür, 2000, p. 249.

60 "A lot of people…": RZA, 2005, p. 191.

60 "If Public Enemy brought…": Tate, 2016, p. 259.

60 "Hip-hop is ancestor…": Tate, 1988, p. 73.

60 "practically exclude the…": *BBC News*, 2016.

60 The irony of the copyright laws: See Mcleod, 2011.

61 The sampling of previously: See Brewster & Broughton, 2006, p. 267.

61 To most of us though: I lifted the term "mediated memories" from José van Dijck.

61 *Memories Don't Live Like People Do*: DJ Honda (featuring

Mos Def), 1998.

61 "Cinematographic and phonographic...": Torlasco, 2013, p. 92.

62 "alien experiences and narratives...": Landsberg, 1992, p. 187.

62 Sampling pushes them: Wershier-Henry, 1995, p. 244.

62 These traces point: Kirschenbaum, 2008, p. 49; As Norman Klein puts it, "a memory 'trace' may satisfy the urge to remember, but not the urge to remember the 'facts'"; 1997, p. 306; For more on traces, memory, and forgetting, see Ricoeur, 2004.

62 "We began to recognize...": Scott, 1982.

63 "prosthetic memories": Landsberg, 1995, p. 175.

63 "something simply lived...": Shusterman, 2000, p. 18.

63 Some argue that: See Lasn, 1999; Pettman writes that "it is as if Walter Benjamin's famous comments concerning the aura have been enlisted by the cinematic apparatus and applied to people, or rather to androids, instead of to works of art"; 2006, p. 174.

63 "[...] technical reproduction can...": Benjamin, 1968, pp. 220-221.

63 When Deckard explains: Landsberg, 1992, p. 185.

63 Although false, the photograph: Bruno, 1990, p. 183; See also Barthes, 1981, p. 65.

63 That is "history": West-Pavlov, 2013, p. 81.

64 "Weak but detectable": Yu, 2010, p. 47.

64 The Celtics call them: Wiener, 2012.

64 "Manifests itself": Yu, 2010, p. 47.

64 Where such photographs: Navas, 2012, p. 13.


64 The remediation of these: Katz, 2004; As David Toop

writes, "Painstaking hours could be spent, using state-of-the-art technology, to make a new track sound authentically old. Somehow, in all the waffle about morality and legality that arose around the subject, the fact that thus was an extraordinary way to compose music was bypassed"; 1999, p. 192.

64 It's not only longing: As Boym writes, "A modern nostalgic can be homesick and sick of home, at once"; 2001, p. 50.

64 If we cannot locate: Bruno, 1990, 190-194.

66 "By consensus, cult members...": Lasn, 1999, p. 53. Roth-Gordon calls this "conversational sampling"; 2009, p. 66.

66 "[Pop] is still considered...": Reynolds, 2011, p. xviii-xix.

66 "The presence of the original...": Benjamin, 1968, p. 220.

66 One of the most distinctive: Mike Davis described *Blade Runner* to Mark Dery as a "gothic romance," adding "*Blade Runner* is a pastiche, and when you peel away some of the layers, its core vision is *Metropolis*, which in turn is Hugh Ferris — this continuing obsession with modernism, where the future city is a kind of monster New York. You could probably go all the way back to a book H.G. Wells wrote in 1906 called *The Future in America*, in which he talks about a methodology for envisioning the end of the 20th century through a process of gigantism. That's what's continuously underlaid that vision — the mile-high skyscrapers, the little squad cars flying around in the air — and *Blade Runner*'s fidelity to this Wellsian vision of the future certainly contrasts Gibson's."; Dery, 1996; See also Anderson, 2016; Davis, 1992; Bukatman, 1993, p. 130; 1997, passim; Klein, 1997, p. 105; Rowley, 2005,

p. 205; Arren, 2017; Pettman, 2006, p. 119.

66 "represent layers of nostalgia...": Klein, 1997, p. 96.

66 Those familiar structures: Bukatman, writes, "*Blade Runner* displays a bold and disturbing extrapolation of current trends: it is a future built upon the detritus of a retrofitted past (our present) in which the city exists as a spectacular site... a future when the only visible monument is a corporate headquarters"; 1993, pp. 130-131.

67 The filmmakers looted: See De Lauzirika, 2007; Sammon, 2017.

### Chapter Four: Spoken Windows

69 "I'll master your...": Tricky, "Christiansands," 1996.

69 "Language itself is a...": Rammellzee, 1985, p. 88.

69 "It's not that I have...": Delany, 1975, p. 11.

69 William Melvin Kelley: Schultz, 2018.

70 Each of our artifacts: Marshall and McLuhan, 1988, p. 3.

70 McLuhan pointed out: McLuhan, 1951.

70 One recent study: See Eisenstein, 2012.

70 The researchers collected tweets: Giles, 2012.

70 The widespread dissemination: Gitlin, 2001.

70 Though Gutenberg's printing: McLuhan, 1964.

71 The telegraph separated: Carey, 1988; See also DeLanda, 1997; Lipsitz, 1990, p. 6; Sconce, 2000.

71 "the Africa within": McLuhan, 1962, p. 45; As abstractly misguided as this sentiment might've been, McLuhan, like Joseph Conrad before him, meant it in the figurative sense; See Dery, 2007.

71 As much as we think: Ong writes, "The evolution of

consciousness through human history is marked by growth in articulate attention to the interior of the individual person as distanced — though not necessarily separated — from the communal structures in which each person is necessarily enveloped"; 1982, p. 174.

71 Think about the difference: Ong continues, "Writing introduces division and alienation, but a higher unity as well. It intensifies the sense of self and fosters more conscious interaction between persons"; 1982, p. 174.

72 "socio-textual community": Pollack, 1998, p. 9.

72 "They're both looking at…": Erwin, J., Malcolm, S. A., Duncan-Mao, A., Matthews, A., Monroe, J., Samuel, A., & Satten, V., 2006.

72 The Middle Passage: Arthur Jafa tells Jace Clayton, "Nam June Paik once said that the culture which will survive in the future is the one you can carry around in your head. Black culture is a profound demonstration of that, because we're strong, traditionally speaking, in the space of what I call immaterial invention, or immaterial expressivity. We came from Africa, where there are 1,000-year-old traditions of material expressivity — sculpture, architecture, etc. But, in the US, we've been defined by the Middle Passage. On a slave ship, all you can take with you is song or rhetoric. You can't take a sculpture or a building with you on a chain gang or to prison. So, that tradition of immaterial expressivity continues. A mix is a perfect example of this because it involves taking pre-existing material and creating new relationships through proximity."; See Clayton, 2018; See also Eshun, 1998, p. 192.

72 As much as it: Benjamin, 1968; Cruz, 2014.

72 The so-named "Hip-Hop Nation": See Alim, 2006; Alim, Ibrahim, & Pennycock, 2009; Fricke & Ahearn, 2002; McLeod, 2016; Omoniyi, 2009; Rose, 1994; Vaidhyanathan, 2001.

72 The figurative language: Gates, 2010; He writes, "Rap is, in other words, a multifarious, multifaceted tradition embedded within African American oral culture that itself shares the rich history of human expression across the ages"; 2010, p. xxv; Greg Tate adds, "The Afro-American tradition has been figurative from its beginnings. How could it have survived otherwise?"; 1992, p. 147; See also Perry, 2012, p. 511.

73 "So many people...": Jay-Z, 2010, p. 55.

73 The signifyin' practice: Burns & Woods, 2018; Williams, 2013.

73 These scripts were: I stole this one from my friend Jason Childers. Thanks, Jason!

73 "When I was...": Jay-Z, 2010, p. 213.

73 "Any hot medium...": McLuhan, 1964, p. 23; Thompson writes, "gaps in lyrical meaning keep listeners immediately involved in the work the music tries to do."; 2005, p. 97.

74 "After Barack was...": Jay-Z, 2010, p. 231.

75 *Rhyme Pays*: Ice-T, 1987.

75 The normal flow: Jakobson, 1960; Feld, 1994.

75 One simple study: McGlone & Tofighbakhsh, 2000.

76 Some argue that: See Gibbs, Jr., 1994; Kövecses, 2000; Lakoff & Johnson, 1980; Ricoueur, 1977.

76 Others argue that: See Nietzsche, 1974; McLeod, 2016.

76 "Where I'm from...": West, 2005.

77 "I'm not a...": Jay-Z, 2005.

77 In one line: See Rose, 2008; Incidentally, Jay-Z's words here echo Rachael's in *Blade Runner* when she says, "I'm not in the business. I *am* the business."

77 "Rap, like oral…": Bradley, 2009, p. 59.

77 Our minds enjoy: Bradley, 2009; See also Empson, 1947.

77 *Let the Rhythm Hit 'Em*: Rakim, 1990.

77 Rhythm is what: Edwards, 2009, p. 111.

77 The rhythm is information: See Lovink, 2002b, p. 350; Williams, 2006, p. XII; Bonilla writes that Gil Scott-Heron's "Whitey on the Moon" and "B Movie" "remain examples of how rhythm and melody can underline uncomfortable truths and deep messages"; Bonilla, 2018, p. 370.

78 In addition, the: Bradley, 2009. For more on rhyme and rhythm techniques, see Edwards, 2009; 2013; RZA, 2005, pp. 210-213; For more on rap as vocal percussion, see Edwards, 2013; 2015.

78 This interplay of: Rakim played saxophone, and says he approached rhyming the same way; see Edwards, 2015, p. 51; See also Brummett, 2004, p. 204.

78 "You know the rhythm…": Public Enemy, 1988.

79 The abolitionist themes: That one's for Greg Tate.

79 It was the first such: Ronda, 1984, p. 310.

80 "It's like when I…": Quoted in Cohen & Krugman, 1996.

80 Allusions activate two: Ben-Porat, 1976, p. 107.

80 These allusions give: Byrne, 2012; Cobb, 2007; Perry, 2004; Potter, 1995.

80 Others see such: Gates, 1988; 2010; Smitherman, 1977.

80 The listened is often: Leppihalme, 1997; Smitherman, 1977.

81 "Hip-hop, an art…": Drake, 2014.

81 Specific cultural allusions: References to other songs within the genre contribute to a horizontal intertext, whereas references to artifacts outside hip-hop are vertically intertextual; See Androutsopoulos, 2009, p. 45-46; Fiske, 1987.

81 For instance, Ice-T once: Ice-T, 1987.

81 "Killers Born Naturally...": Def & Kweli, 1998.

82 "Rap's signature characteristic...": Gates, 2010, p. xxiv.

82 Their interactions are: Gorham & Gilligan, 2006.

82 They may involve: See Roudiez, 1980.

82 Allusion is a broader: Hutcheon, 1985.

82 Some see allusion: See Pasco, 1994; Lacasse, 2000.

82 In addition, the term: Irwin, 2004; Roudiez, 1980.

82 "the transposition of one...": Roudiez, 1980, p. 15; Italics in original. Some rhetoricians refer to one-to-one intertextuality as "merging" and intertextuality involving multiple sources as "sampling."; See Luker, 2003; Vail, 2006.

82 Using allusion to designate: Perry, 2004, p. 36.

83 Identifying others with: Gorham & Gilligan, 2006; Leppihalme, 1997.

83 An audience member's: de Certeau, 1984; Jenkins, 1992; 2006.

83 "I am whatever...": Eminem, 2000.

83 "I'm the R to the A...": Rakim, 1986; Nas interpolates this lyric as well, rapping, "I'm the N to the A to the S-I-R. If I wasn't then I must've been Escobar."; Nas, 2001; Perry cites these allusions as another intertextual layer of rap's call-and-response between emcee and audience; See Perry, 2004, p. 36.

84 *Subversive Scripts*: dälek, 2007.

84 The lines blur here: Uchill, 2015.

84 Using allusion as a game: boyd & Marwick, 2011, p. 22; Steganography was used in World War II. The Russians painted railroad tracks on the tops of trains so that they couldn't be seen from the air; see Guffey, 2015; See also Wayner, 2009.

85 Taking the concept: Butler, 1990; Magnus, 2006.

85 By employing obscure: Geert Lovink calls this "public secrecy." See Lovink, 2002b, p. 356; Barbara Franz adds, "Rap is the ideal medium for this form of resistance."; Franz, 2015, p. 89.

85 Alienating anyone outside: Krims, 2000; Negas, 2004; Shusterman, 2004.

86 It could be: Perry, 2004.

86 The Five Percent Nation: Allah, 2007; Knight, 2007.

86 Though they reject: Miyakawa, 2003; Allah, 2007; Knight, 2007.

86 From Rakim to RZA: As dream hampton writes, "black gods calling whitey devil, even in William Gibson speak, has always brought out the Norman Mailer in whiteboys."; See hampton, 1998.

86 "Ninety-three million miles...": Wu-Tang Clan, 1997; See RZA, 2005, p. 158.

86 "Brief references...": Miyakawa, 2005, p. 72.

87 "March of the wooden soldiers...": Wu-Tang Clan, 1997; See RZA, 2005, p. 157.

87 These allusive expression: See Allen, Jr., 1996, pp. 159-191; Miyakawa, 2003, pp. 171-185.

87 Oppression never: Lipari, 2013, p. 131-132; Scott, 2003.

87 "The theatrical imperatives...": Scott, 2003, p. 4.

88 However, many acts: Gaines, 1999.

88 *Boundary Functions*: Kaczynski, 1967.

88 "Texts are complex...": Brummett, 2008, p. 118; See also Kehinde, 2011.

88 "communities of practice": Wenger, 1999, passim.

89 Boundary objects can be: Star and Griesemer, 1989; Wenger, 1999, p. 105.

89 "Just as graffiti writers...": Rose, 1994, p. 82.

*Chapter Five: The Process of Illumination*

91 "Gothic's obsession with...": Davenport-Hines, 1998, p. 3-4.

91 "From the moment...": Tate, 2016, p. 335-336.

91 "Darkness has its...": Rammellzee, 1990, p. 29.

92 "The Romans stole the...": Rammellzee, 1986.

92 Set the Controls... Pink Floyd, 1968.

92 "All four of us...": Quoted in McLeod, 2015, p. 88.

92 "At that point...": Quoted in Kahn, 2006, p. 230.

93 The most famous African-American: See Stanley, 2014, pp. 27-33.

93 Herman, which in: Stanley, 2014, p. 167.

93 Sun Ra rejected white: Schriber, 2013, p. 39; See also Clayton, 2016, p. 13.

94 These can't be viewed: See Dery, 1993.

94 "I never heard Sun Ra...": Interview with Labtekwon, July 10, 2017; On "Dawn in Luxor" from Shabazz Palaces' *Lese Majesty*, Ish Butler says, "They couldn't lull us, so they synthesize our realness."

94 Contention has followed: Mark Dery himself, in naming

this "Afrofuturism," does so, "for want of a better term." See Dery, 1993, p. 736; Dery, 1994, p. 180; For rather unproductive critiques of this coinage, see Rose, 2014 and Lavender, 2015.

94 "[T]he legacy of Black people...": Interview with Labtekwon, July 10, 2017.

95 "They had a movie...": Sun Ra, 2006, p. 12; Richard Pryor has a joke based on the same sentiment, but he adds, "That's why we gotta make movies. Then we be in the pictures."; Pryor, 1976; Eshun inserts Sun Ra into *Blade Runner*, calling him "the Tyrell Corporation's unseen director"; 1998, p. 155.

95 The core assumption: See Bould, 2007.

95 "You've outlived the Bible...": Quoted in Lock, 1999, p. 41; Sun Ra regularly claimed it was after the end of the world in his live shows; See Corbett, 1994, p. 22; Eshun, 1998, p. 155.

95 "I believe the first...": Quoted in Tate, 2016, p. 132

95 This is our story: Lock writes that in slaves' mythic worlds, "'home' can symbolize both the mythic future and the mythic past"; 1999, p. 42; Paul Gilroy calls these two processes the "politics of transformation" and "politics of fulfilment." See Gilroy, 1993, passim.

95 "[...] just as the slaves...": Lock, 1999, p. 40.

96 The African-American experience: See Edwards, 2011; Eshun, 1998, p. 192; Quinn, 2013; Womack, 2013; Greg Tate describes Richard Wright's *Invisible Man* (1952): "The whole intellectual landscape of the novel, which deals with the condition of being alien and alienated, speaks, in a sense, to the way in which being black in America is a science fiction experience"; quoted in Dery,

1994, p. 208; Grace Jones writes of her early modeling days in Paris: "They wanted to get to know me because I was like an alien who had landed from outer space."; Jones, 2015, p. 115; Lee "Scratch" Perry claimed to be "an alien from another world, from outta space... I live in space. I'm only a visitor here"; Quoted in Heath, 1997. Even Tricky says, "I feel alien, and like someone's going to recognize me in a minute as an alien."; Quoted in Reynolds, 1995.

96 With its Off-World colonies: Sean Redmond writes, "This type of racial coding is structured into the very spatial organization of the film, so that the people of race populate the lower levels of the city, while the white people live in the higher levels, or have moved off-world all together, abandoning a city/planet they see as having been taken over by the racial other."; 2003, p. 56; See also Desser, 1991; Green, 2003; Sinker, 1992. And after all, Replicant or regular man, Deckard is still a fucking cop.

96 "accelerated decrepitude": Fancher & Peoples, 1982.

96 "the state-sanctioned...": Gilmore, 2002, p. 261.

96 "I can't pay no doctor bills...": Scott-Heron, 1970.

97 Unlike most ancient: See Charroux, 1974, pp. 29-30.

98 Similarly, contemporary monastic: Von Däniken, 1968, p. 151.

98 "The powerful employ...": Eshun, 2003, p. 289.

98 As skeptical as it: Eshun, 2013.

99 Saucer Wisdom: Rucker, 1999.

99 Idaho pilot Kenneth Arnold: Arnold, 1952; Lacitis, 2017.

99 Roughly fifty years later: hampton, 2006.

99 In the most oversimplified: See Hinds, 2002, p. 157.

99 "Every serious artist hopes…": Personal correspondence with Mudede, May 7, 2017.

100 "That song title was part…": Quoted in Coleman, 2007, p. 169-170.

101 After having released one: In her review of the record, dream hampton writes, ""Dial 7 (Axioms of Creamy Spies)," *Blowout*'s most perfect track, is more than a spoof on Blaxploitation films; it's a cool cat's guide to guerrilla warfare. And fuck it, if myth of action is all I'm gonna get out of this culture we call hip-hop, then give me more choruses that tell eighth-graders that the almighty man ain't shit."; See hampton, 1994.

101 "I like the alien aspect…": Interview with Ishmael Butler, January 26, 2017.

102 Frantz Fanon maintained that: Fanon wrote, "Scientific objectivity had to be ruled out, since the alienated and the neurotic were my brother, my sister, my father. I constantly tried to demonstrate to the black man that in a sense he abnormalizes himself, and to the white man that he is both mystifier and mystified"; 1967, p. 200; The term "graffiti" was even contested by legendary practitioners like Phase 2 and Rammellzee; See Galli, 2009; Gill, 2014.

102 The Other or the alien: Ta-Nehisi Coates writes, "… race is the child of racism, not the father. And the process of naming 'the people' has never been a matter of genealogy and physiognomy so much as one of hierarchy"; 2015, p. 7; Or, as Fred Moten puts it, "Blackness isn't a people problem; it's a problemitization of the people."; 2017, p. 202; See also Chambers, 1976; Weheliye, 2014; Womack, 2016.

103 Acts are corralled: Chang, 2005.

103 *Tales from the Rails*: Lordz of Brooklyn (featuring Rammellzee), 1995.

103 "The graffiti on the subway...": Rucker, 1999, p. 159.

104 "They give you a name...": Quoted in Chalfant & Silver, 1983.

104 Branding and advertising are: On the origins of graffiti, Joe Austin writes, "The proliferation of posters, advertisements, and signs bearing the images and names of products and proprietors in twentieth-century cities is one obvious place to begin. These are the directly visible extensions of individual/corporate identities into the new shared urban public spaces of the streets, a quantitatively and qualitatively new site in human history where hundreds of thousands of often spectacularly displayed names abound, each intent upon catching the eyes of potential consumers and imprinting itself on their memories. Whatever its particulars, every advertising sign broadcasts at least one common message: 'Don't forget this name'."; 2001,p. 39; See also, Miller, 2002, p. 144-181; As David Byrne puts it, "I am an advertisement for a version of myself."; Quoted in Poster, 1997, p. 201.

104 "Long before low-wattage...": Cobb, 2007, p. 3.

104 "Their efforts paved...": Tate, 2016, p. 127.

104 "I don't care about nobody...": Quoted in Chalfant & Silver, 1983.

105 "[...] ads are not intended...": McLuhan, 1970, p. 48; Underlining in original.

105 This most public...: In the graffiti-themed Company

Flow song, "Lune TNS" Big Juss says that if you "don't understand, obviously this wasn't made for you. So, fuck you."

105 "Ours was a world...": Phase 2, 1996, p. 55.

105 "Historically speaking...": KRS-One, 1995.

105 Like Gladys Glover: See Kanin, 1954.

106 The painted caves are: Austin, 2001, p. 41.

106 It's ambient imagery: Citing Jean Baudrillard, Gary Genosko writes that graffiti writers "'volatilize' the code and exist beyond the communicative grid," adding "They are not decipherable like a commercial message." See Genosko, 2012, pp. 86-87; Baudrillard, 1981, p. 184.

106 "The magic of...": Quoted in McLuhan & Nevitt, 1972, p. 92.

106 Alpha-Positive, a secretary: For pictures of these get-ups, see Freddy, 2011, pp. 90-95; Jacobson, 2013, pp. 100-101; James, 2013, p. 37; Rammellzee, 1990; Sonaike & Werner, 2009, pp. 08-13.

107 "They are in the vein...": Tate, 2016, p. 130.

107 "Rammellzee is alien material...": Butler interview, January 26, 2017.

107 "It is not to be told...": Quoted in Kennedy, 2010.

107 He was able to freestyle: Haj-Najafu, 2010.

107 He explained graffiti: Witten & White, 2001, p. 76.

107 "part street physics professor...": Freddy, 2011, p. 90.

107 His 1983 single: See McCormick, 2012; Tate, 2010, pp. 127-136; Tompkins, 2010, passim; Sonaike & Werner, 2009, p. 08-13;

108 "Rammellzee was the Sun Ra...": Quoted in Rosen, 2018.

108 The single is a certified: Berger, 2012.

108 "Rammellzee is on purpose...": Quoted in Tompkins, 2012.

108 Rammellzee considered Sun Ra: Tate, 2016, p. 133.

108 "I see that society is...": Quoted in Miller, 2002, p. 59.

109 Graffiti is a tradition: As Robert Farris Thompson writes, "It is not just the act of taking over space that characterizes the urban African American sensibilities in aerosol art, it is the approach to rhythm, color, style, multiple naming; the use of the train as a metaphor; and the creation of a culture of resistance to official narratives"; Quoted in Miller, 2002, p. 5; Rammellzee described a part of a tag to Ivor Miller as a "harponic whip launcher," to which Miller adds that he was "depicting stylized symbols as weapons in a battle over identity and representation."; Miller, 2002, p. 85; See also Hebdige, 1979; Tompkins, 2013.

109 "The piece itself...": Quoted in Tate, 2016, p. 131.

109 "The letter is armed...": Quoted in deAK, 1983, p. 91.

109 "The graffiti artists of...": Quoted in Sonaike & Werner, 2009, p. 10.

109 In Rammellzee's view: Miller, 2002, p. 90.

109 "From the fourth century...": Rammellzee, 1979/2003; All-capitals in original.

110 "'RΔMM' is Raamses...": Quoted in Miller, 2002, p. 86.

110 "These are alien shapes!": Butler interview, January 26, 2017.

110 "The genetic code...": Quoted in Galli, 2008, p. 118.

111 "All of my art...": Quoted in Tate, 2016, p. 134.

111 Separated from their linguistic: Jacobson, 2013.

111 In addition to: Miller, 2002, p. 191, n 5.

111 "We're advanced in terms...": Quoted in Tate, 2016,

p. 136; My italics.

111 Anything you could do: Daniel Dennett once used this phrase to describe Douglas Hofstadter. See Dennett, 1998, p. 236.

112 *Long Live the New Flesh*: This subhead is taken from the premier body-horror film, *Videodrome*; Cronenberg, 1983.

112 "Meeting Ramm in person...": Personal correspondence with Juice Aleem, June 13, 2018.

113 "You call me an...": Quoted in Galli, 2009, p. 121.

113 "Instead Goths celebrate...": Davenport-Hines, 1998, p. 7.

113 "His energy has just...": Quoted in Kennedy, 2010.

### *Chapter Six: Let Bygones Be Icons*

115 "Tape-recorders...": Durgnat, 1971, p. 233.

115 "What used to...": Ras Kass, 2001.

115 "Anything dead coming...": Morrison, 1987, p. 35.

116 "An English clergyman...": Quoted in Neale, 2000; The clergyman's diary anecdote is in Jennings, 1985; See also, Goodman, 2010, pp. 18-20; Josiffe, 2018.

116 "If our personality...": Quoted in Gardner, 2001, p. 213; See also Josiffe, 2018.

116 One of the characters: Cavallaro, 2000.

117 "When the construct...": Gibson, 1984, p. 104.

117 Using the studio: David Toop calls recording a "dream-text, a vision of possible worlds"; Toop, 1995, p. 275.

117 "The first time...": Jay-Z, 2010, p. 5.

117 The space between: Bailey, 2011; Blackman, 2011.

118 "They damaged his nervous...": Gibson, 1984, p. 6.

118 The body is the site: de Certeau writes, "There is no law that is not inscribed on bodies. Every law has a hold on the body"; 1984, p. 139; See also Foucault, 1977; Browne, 2015.

119 "It is because of this nexus...": Chude-Sokei, 2016, p. 148.

119 Seemingly confused: See Rapatzikou, 2004.

119 While both genres: Aldiss, 2001, p. 19; Aldiss, 1995, p. 78; Botting, 1996, p. 101; Clute & Nicholls, 1993, p. 154; Davenport-Hines, 1998, p. 190; Gledhill, 2017, p. 219; Hogle, 2002, p. xix; Punter & Byron, 2004, p. 199; Stephanou, 2017, p. 234; Young, 2008.

119 Monsters like the one: Waldby, 2002; Shildrick, 1996.

119 And like any good: Stephanou, 2017.

119 "The novel both...": Waldby, 2002, p. 29.

120 New York's Big L cited: Kangas, 2013.

120 "Gangsta rap had already...": Quoted in Coleman, 2014.

121 "stock characters in a neoliberal...": Burton, 2017, p. 7.

121 "Okay, first things first...": Minaj, 2010.

121 "space for the alterity...": Khair, 2009, p. 146; Italics in original; See also, Chude-Sokei, 2016; Monk, 2006, pp. 267-304.

121 In the face of irreconcilable: Khair, 2009, p. 132.

121 Twin infinitives: Hagerty & Herrema, 1990.

121 He died on September 13: Frank Alexander, one of Tupac's bodyguards said, "It was like a spaceship had beamed down, snatched him, and took him away. It was that fast."; Quoted in Westhoff, 2016, p. 345.

121 Six months later: Kinnon, 1997.

121 The two had been embroiled: Chang, 2005; Wang, 2006.

122 Hip-hop is haunted: See Cooper, 2004, p. 237; The list is long and unfortunately getting longer, including Jam Master Jay, Guru, Ol' Dirty Bastard, Big L, Big Pun, Eazy-E, Freaky Tah, Adam Yauch, Proof, Pimp C, Sean Price, Prodigy, Phife Dawg, Roc Raida,      Mac Miller, and others. Rest in peace, all.

122 "A dead emcee is…": Neate, 2003, p. 16.

122 "Criminal records sell…": Harkness, 2014, p. 197.

122 Criminals with permanent records: As Walter Benjamin pointed out about such a public criminal, "however repellent his ends may have been, has aroused the secret admiration of the public."; 1978, p. 281.

122 Having found second: Of these hauntings, Hillel Schwartz (1996) writes that sampling "ultimately erases the line between the quick and the dead"; 1996, p. 311; John Durham Peters adds that mediated communication via recording "is ultimately indistinguishable from communication with the dead"; 1999, p. 276; He also points out that the phonograph "is a medium that preserves ghosts that would otherwise be evanescent"; 1999, p. 160; Simon Reynolds writes, "Cassettes could be considered a hauntological format because, like the scratches and surface noise on vinyl, the hiss of tape noise reminds you constantly that this is a recording. But cassettes are a ghost medium in the sense that as far as mainstream culture is concerned, they are dead, an embarrassing relic."; Reynolds, 2011, p. 350; See also, Derrida, 1994, p. 63; Hip-hop is hella haunted.

122 "Rappers who sample…": Williams, 2013, p. 109.

122 Kendrick Lamar caught: "Humble" shares as much with

Tyler, the Creator's "Yonkers" as it does with Wopo's "Elm Street."

123 Like Tupac and Biggie: Jimmy Wopo was 2-months old when Biggie was killed.

123 *Rock My Hologram*: Aleem, 2009.

124 "Hov got flow though...": Jay-Z, 2010, p. 98.

124 Much as Malcolm X: Hess, 2007.

124 Tupac envisioned his own: Hinds writes, "Tupac was an ember in constant search of a bonfire. Las Vegas proved the final conflagration."; 2002, p. 109.

125 The effect debuted: For the Pepper's ghost's uses in theatre, see Huhtamo, 2013; Pepper, 1996; Writing about the effect in early film, David J. Jones writes, "Thus, only months into cine-history, the Gothic machine encoded (and encoding) in diverse media reasserted itself as a subset in cinematography. The jokes and parody in this film, the ridiculous band of traipsing ghosts and sudden transformations cannot quite banish the chill of some of the effects in which the Gothic lingers on."; 2011, p. 114; For Tupac's Coachella appearance specifically, see Fusco, 2015; McLeod, 2016.

125 "the spectralization of a live...": Jones, 2011, p. 89.

125 The DJ converges: Katz, 2004.

126 Tupac's hologram brought: As Mike Ladd puts it, "New Gods are created every TV season in this country, living, mythological characters. Viewing celebrities in this way is not new. But viewing celebrities who have been executed, or physically reconstructed, seemed to be a true embrace of a post-futurist perspective with all its horror and promise"; 2003, p. 106-107.

126 In the summer: Parker & Quinn, 2015.

126 The young rapper: Krzeczowski, 2018.

126 "Chicago, we need...": Quoted in Coscarelli, 2015.

126 "I know nothing...": Quoted in Coscarelli, 2015.

126 Just as Tupac's hologram: Zadeh writes, "Holograms have already been pretty damn impressive in bringing stars back from the dead, but the notion of a rapper projecting his hologram into states where he is wanted for arrest is the kind of super futuristic law-defying shit that would get William Gibson so hyped, he'd need to put a small cushion on his lap to save embarrassment."; Zadeh, 2015.

127 *A Ghost is Born*: Tweedy, 2004.

127 When we hear voices: Quoting Philip Auslander in their discussion of haunting in music, Shaffer and Gunn argue, "'listeners do not perceive recorded music as disembodied'. Rather, he argues that listeners and performers fashion a 'fictional body' or personae when listening to music, an imaginary corporeality that is ultimately associated with a 'real person'"; Shafer & Gunn, 2006, p. 44. See also Rotman, 2008, p. xiii.

127 When it comes: See Toop, 1995; Josiffe, 2018.

127 The book includes: See Raudive, 1971.

127 On one, the: Raudive, 1971, p. 149.

128 "Sonja L., my friend...": Raudive, 1971, p. 43.

128 "Be ready, even...": Raudive, 1971, p. 43.

128 Just as the Church: See Bander, 1972.

128 "If these be...": Quoted in Bander, 1972, p. 104.

128 One of Gibson's: Gibson, 2003, p. 115.

128 Describing the onset: See Mishara, 2010.

128 "specific experience of...": See Brugger, 2001.

129 Are they patterns: Hayles refers to virtual bodies as "a

pattern rather than a presence"; Hayles, 1999, p. 25 and passim.

129 "[T]he recorded voices...": McLeod, 2016, p. 114.

129 "In hip-hop, no higher...": Allen, 2000, p. 91.

129 "We usually think...": Shaviro, 2010, pp. 66-67; See also Gordon, 1997, p. 64; Kleinberg, 2017.

### Chapter Seven: Return to Cinder

131 "The matches have been...": Rammellzee, 1990, p. 3.

131 "We will either...": Jünger, 1992.

131 "The moment of real poetry...": Quoted in Marcus, 1989, p. 24.

132 If you think of: As Alan Kay says, "Technology is anything that wasn't around when you were born"; quoted in Greelish, 2013.

132 "in between P.M. Dawn...": Quoted in Eagle, 2017.

132 "These endlessly replicating...": Shaviro, 2004, p. 64.

133 They study these: Quoted in Gwinn, 2014, p. 181.

133 Gibson says *Neuromancer*: Quoted in Long, 2007, p. 68.

133 those without will: Rosenfeld & Messner, 1997.

133 Hip-hop is a bridge: Hal Foster might call this a "simulated bohemia."; Foster, 1985, p. 35.

134 "To the extent that...": Quoted in Doctorow, 2014, p. 154.

134 Authenticity comes from: Hess, 2012, p. 644.

134 "We must find and...": RZA, 2009, p. 175; RZA goes one to say, "You're slaves to the past, to nostalgia. You're blind to what's right in front of you."; 2009, p. 198.

135 *Black Velocities*: Bradbury, 1950, p. 32.

135 Cyberpunk might be: See Zadeh, 2015.

135 The promised land: Lipari, 2013, pp. 119-120.

136 "The Earth is layer...": brown, 2017, p. 49.

136 "We wield 'science fiction' voice...": Metropolarity, 2016, p. 3.

136 "Our neighborhoods, our networks...": Metropolarity, 2016, p. 5.

137 Sun Ra once said: Lock, 1989.

137 "Perhaps the most...": brown, 2017, p. 49.

137 "We're the ghost of 1990s...": Téllez, 2016, p. 46.

137 "You have to forge...": Téllez, 2016, p. 20.

137 Hackers of all kinds: See Aleem, 2016, p. 14.

# BIBLIOGRAPHY

Adler, Bill. (1999). "Bill Adler's Top 5 Mainstream Media Rap Coverage Travesties." In Sacha Jenkins, Elliott Wilson, Chairman Mao, Gabriel Alvarez, & Brent Rollins (Eds.), *Ego Trip's Book of Rap Lists*. New York: Ego Trip Publications.

Adler, Jerry. (1990, March 19). "The Rap Attitude." *Newsweek,* CXV, 12, pp. 56-59.

Aldiss, Brian. *The Detached Retina: Aspects of SF and Fantasy.* (1995). Syracuse, NY: Syracuse University Press.

Aldiss, Brian. (2001). *Trillion Year Spree* (with David Wingrove) (1986). New York: House of Stratus.

Aleem, Juice. (2016) *Afrofutures and Astro-Black Travel: A Passport to a Melanated Future.* London: Juice Aleem

Ali, Lorraine. (1996, October). The Tricky Question. *Option.* pp. 74-81.

Alim, H. Samy. (2006). *Roc the Mic Right: The Language of Hip-Hop Culture.* New York: Routledge.

Alim, H. Samy, Ibraham, Awad, & Pennycock, Alastair. (2009). *Global Linguistic Flows: Hip-hop Cultures, Youth Identities, and the Politics of Language.* New York: Routledge.

Allen, Jr., Ernest. (1996). Making the Strong Survive: The Contours and Contradictions of Message Rap. In William Eric Perkins (Ed.), *Droppin' Science: Critical Essays on Rap Music and Hip-hop Culture.* Philadelphia, PA: Temple University Press, pp. 159-191.

Allen, Graham. (2000). *Intertextuality: The New Critical Idiom*. New York: Routledge.

Allen, Harry. (2000). "Hip-Hop Hi-Tech." In Kevin Powell (Ed.), *Step into a World: A Global Anthology of the New Black Literature* (pp. 91-95). New York: John Wiley & Sons.

Ambrosch, Gerfried. (2018). *The Poetry of Punk: The Meaning Behind Punk Rock and Hardcore Lyrics*. New York: Routledge.

Anderson, Darran. (2016, February 4) What Cyberpunk Was and What it Will Be. *Killscreen*. Retrieved on April 26, 2017 from https://killscreen.com/versions/what-cyberpunk-was-and-what-it-will-be/

Anderson, Erika M. (2014). 2014: The Year Cyberpunk Broke. *Pitchfork*. Retrieved on March 17, 2017 from http://pitchfork.com/thepitch/576-op-ed-2014-the-year-that-cyberpunk-broke/

Androutsopoulos, Jannis. (2009). Language and the Three Spheres of Hip-Hop. In H. H. Samy Alim, Awad Ibrahim, & Alastair Pennycook (Eds.), *Global Linguistic Flows: Hip-hop Cultures, Youth Identities, and the Politics of Language* (pp. 43-62). New York: Routledge.

Arcenillas, Javier. (2018). *UFO Presences*. Barcelona, Spain: RM Verlag, S.L.

Arnold, Kenneth (with Raymond A. Palmer). (1952). *The Coming of the Saucers: A Documentary Report on Sly Objects That Have Mystified the World*. Amherst, WI: Ray Palmer.

Attali, Jacques. (1977): *Noise: The Political Economy of Music*. Minneapolis, MN: University of Minnesota Press.

Austin, Joe. (2001). *Taking the Train: How Graffiti Art Became an Urban Crisis in New York City*. New York: Columbia University Press.

Atewa, Camae. (2016). *Fetish Bones*. Philadelphia, PA: Afro-Futurist Affair/House of Future Sciences Books.

Bailey, Julius. (2011). *Jay-Z: Essays on Hip-Hop's Philosopher King*. Jefferson, NC: McFarland.

Ball, Jared. (2011). *I Mix What I Like: A Mixtape Manifesto*. Oakland, CA: AK Press.

Bander, Peter. (1972). *Carry on Talking: How Dead Are the Voices?* Gerrards Cross, Buckinghamshire: Colin Smythe Ltd.

Barthes, Roland. (1981). *Camera Lucida: Reflections on Photography*. New York: Hill and Wang.

Bascunan, Rodrigo, (2016). *Hip-Hop Evolution*. Directed by Darby Wheeler, Sam Dunn & Scot McFadyen. Los Angeles: Banger Films.

Batey, Angus. (2010, October 7). The Hip-Hop Heritage Society. *The Guardian*. London. Retrieved on April 22, 2017 from https://www.theguardian.com/music/2010/oct/07/hiphop-heritage-public-enemy-krs-one

Baudrillard, Jean. (1981). Requiem for the Media. In *For a Critique of the Political Economy of the Sign*, trans. Charles Levin. New York: Telos.

*BBC News*. (2016, May 31). "Kraftwerk Loses German Hip-Hop Copyright Case in Top Court." Retrieved on July 11, 2016 from http://www.bbc.com/news/world-europe-36415880

Benjamin, Walter. (1968). The Work of Art in the Age of Mechanical Reproduction. In *Illuminations*. London: Fontana, pp. 217–252.

Benjamin, Walter. (1978). *Reflections: Essays, Aphorisms, and Autobiographical Writings*. New York: Harcourt Brace.

Benjamin, Walter. (1989). Paris, capitale du XIXe siècle (1939). In *Le vivre des Passages*, J. Lacoste (trans.). Cerf, Paris.

Benjamin, Walter. (1999). *The Arcades Project*. Cambridge: Belknap Press.

Berger, Aaron. (2012, September 25). Rammellzee's Singular Visual Stylings. *Beautiful/Decay*. Retrieved on March 11, 2017 from http://www.beautifuldecay.com/2012/09/25/rammellzees-singular-visual-stylings/

Bergier, Jacques. (1973). *Extraterrestrial Visitations from Prehistoric Times to the Present*. New York: Signet.

Ben-Porat, Ziva. (1976). The Poetics of Literary Allusion. *PTL: A Journal for Descriptive Poetics and Theory of Literature, Volume 1*. Amsterdam: North-Holland Publishing Company.

Bethke, Bruce. (1983, November). Cyberpunk. *Amazing Science Fiction Stories*, Volume 57, Number 4.

Blackman, Toni. (2011). Jigga Speaks: The Tradition of Black Oratorical Genius. In Bailey (Ed.), *Jay-Z: Essays on Hip-Hop's Philosopher King*. Jefferson, NC: McFarland. pp. 25-38.

Blake, Victoria. (2013). Introduction. In *Cyberpunk: Stories of Hardware, Software, Wetware, Revolution, and Evolution*. Portland, OR: Underland Press.

Blistein, Jon. (2016, May 31). Kraftwerk Lose Copyright Case in German High Court. *Rolling Stone*. Retrieved on July 11, 2016 from https://www.rollingstone.com/music/music-news/kraftwerk-lose-copyright-case-in-german-high-court-53007/

Blumrich, Josef F. (1974). *The Spaceships of Ezekiel*. New York: Bantam.

Bonger, William. (1969). *Criminality and Economic Conditions*. Bloomington, IN: Indiana University Press.

Bonilla, Eddie. (2018). Proto-Rap. In the *St. James Encyclopedia of Hip-Hop Culture*. Detroit, MI: Gale Cengage.

Booker, M. Keith (Ed.). (2014). *Comics through Time: A History of Icons, Idols, and Ideas* (vol. 3). Westport, CT: Greenwood Publishing.

Bould, Mark. (2007, July). The Ships Landed Long Ago: Afrofuturism and Black SF. *Science Fiction Studies*, vol 34, pt. 2.

boyd, danah & Marwick, Alice E. (2011, September 22). Social Privacy in Networked Publics: Teens' Attitudes, Practices, and Strategies. Paper presented at Oxford Internet Institute's A Decade in Internet Time: Symposium on the Dynamics of the Internet and Society, Oxford, England.

Boym, Svetlana. (2001). *The Future of Nostalgia*. New York: Basic Books.

Bradbury, Ray. (1950). *The Martian Chronicles*. New York: Doubleday.

Bradley, Adam. (2009). *Book of Rhymes: The Poetics of Hip-Hop*. New York: Basic Books.

Bradley, Adam & DuBois, Andrew (Eds.). (2010). *The Anthology of Rap*. New Haven, CT: Yale University Press.

Braidotti, Rosi. (2013). *The Posthuman*. Cambridge: Polity.

Brewster, Bill & Broughton, Frank (2006). *Last Night a DJ Saved My Life: The History of the Disc Jockey*. London: Headline.

brown, adrienne maree. (2017). *Emergent Strategy: Shaping Change, Changing Worlds*. Chico, CA: AK Press.

Brown, Mark. (2012, October 18). Record Companies Feed Off Violence. *Chicago Sun-Times*, p. 5.

Browne, Simone. (2015). *Dark Matters: On the Surveillance of Blackness*. Durham, NC: Duke University Press.

Brugger, Peter. (2001). From Haunted Brain to Haunted Science: A Cognitive Neuroscience View of Paranormal and Pseudoscientific Thought. In J. Houran and R. Lange (Eds.). *Hauntings and Poltergeists: Multidisciplinary Perspectives*. North Carolina: McFarland & Company, Inc. Publishers.

Brummett, Barry. (2008). *A Rhetoric of Style*. Carbondale, IL: Southern Illinois University Press.

Brummett, Barry. (2004). *Rhetoric in Popular Culture*. New York: St. Martin's.

Bruno, Giuliana. (1990). Ramble City: Postmodernism and Blade Runner. In Annette Kuhn (Ed.), *Alien Zone: Cultural Theory and Contemporary Science Fiction Cinema*. New York: Verso. pp. 183-195.

Bukatman, Scott. (1993). *Terminal Identity: The Virtual Subject in Postmodern Science Fiction*. Durham, NC: Duke University Press.

Bukatman, Scott. (1997). *BFI Film Classics: Blade Runner*. London: British Film Institute.

Burns, Lori & Woods, Alyssa. (2018). Rap Gods and Monsters: Words, Music, and Images in the Hip-hop Intertexts of Eminem, Jay-Z, and Kanye West. In Lori Burns & Serge LaCasse (Eds.), *The Pop Palimpsest: Intertextuality in Recorded Popular Music*. Ann Arbor, MI: University of Michigan Press. pp. 215-251.

Burton, Justin Adams. (2017). *Posthuman Rap*. New York: Oxford University Press.

Butler, Andrew M. (2000). *Cyberpunk: The Pocket Essential*. North Pomfret, VT: Trafalgar Square.

Butler, Judith. (1990). *Gender Trouble: Feminism and the Subversion of Identity*. New York: Routledge.

Byrne, David. (2012). *How Music Works*. San Francisco: McSweeney's.

Campbell, Robert L. & Trent, Christopher (Eds.). (1994). *The Earthly Recordings of Sun Ra*. Redwood, NY: Cadence Jazz Books.

Caramanica, Jon. (2012, October 4). Chicago Hip-Hop's Burst of Change. *The New York Times*. https://www.nytimes.com/2012/10/07/arts/music/chicago-hip-hops-raw-burst-of-change.html

Carey, James W. (1988). *Communication as Culture: Essays on Media and Society*. New York: HarperCollins.

Carrington, André M. (2016). *Speculative Blackness: The Future of Race in Science Fiction*. Minneapolis, MN: University of Minnesota.

Castleman, Craig. (1982). *Getting Up: Subway Graffiti in New York*. Cambridge, MA: MIT Press.

Cavallaro, Dani. (2000). *Cyberpunk and Cyberculture: Science Fiction and the Work of William Gibson*. London: The Althone Press.

Chalfant, Henry. (1983). *Style Wars*. Directed by Tony Silver. [DVD]. New York: Public Art Films.

Chambers, Iain. (1976). A Strategy for Living: Black Music and White Subcultures. In Stuart Hall & Tony Jefferson (Eds.), *Resistance Through Rituals: Youth Subcultures in Post-War Britain*. New York: Routledge. pp. 157-166.

Chambers, Iain. (1986). *Popular Culture: The Metropolitan Experience*. New York: Routledge.

Chambers, Iain, (1997). Maps, Movies, Music, and Memory. In David B. Clarke (Ed.), *The Cinematic City*. New York: Routledge. pp. 233-244.

Chang, Jeff. (2005). *Can't Stop, Won't Stop: A History of the Hip-Hop Generation*. New York: Picador.

Chang, Jeff. (2006). *Total Chaos: The Art and Aesthetics of Hip-hop*. New York: Basic Civitas.

Charroux, Robert. (1974). *The Mysterious Past*. London: Futura Publications Ltd.

*Chart Attack*. (2006, September 18). 'My Sharona" Writers Sue Run-DMC for Sampling "It's Tricky." Retrieved on November 10, 2013 from http://www.chartattack.com/news/2006/09/18/my-sharona-writers-sue-run-dmc-for-sampling-its-tricky/ archived at https://web.archive.org/web/20171221105055/http://www.chartattack.com:80/news/2006/09/18/my-sharona-writers-sue-run-dmc-for-sampling-its-tricky

Chavez. (1996). *Ride the Fader*. [CD] New York: Matador Records.

Chude-Sokei, Louis. (2016). *The Sound of Culture: Diaspora and Black Technopoetics*. Middletown, CT: Wesleyan.

Clayton, Jace. (2016). *Uproot: Travels in 21st-Century Music and Digital Culture*. New York: Farrar, Straus and Giroux.

Clayton, Jace. (2018, February 22). As Brilliant as the Sun. *Frieze*. Retrieved March 8, 2018 from https://frieze.com/article/brilliant-sun

Clute, John & Nicholls, Peter (1993). Mary W. Shelley. In *Encyclopedia of Science Fiction*. Orbit/Time Warner Book Group UK.

Coates, Na-Tehesi. (2015). *Between the World and Me*. New York: Spiegel & Grau.

Cobb, William Jelani. (2007). *To the Break of Dawn: A Freestyle on the Hip-Hop Aesthetic*. New York: NYU Press.

Cohen, Jason & Krugman, Michael. (1996, October). The Madness of King Tricky. *Raygun*.

Colbert, Soyica Diggs. (2014). Black Movements: Flying Africans in Spaceships. In Thomas F. DeFrantz & Anita Gonzalez (Eds.), *Black Performance Theory*. Durham, NC: Duke University Press. pp. 129-148.

Coleman, Brian. (2005). *Rakim Told Me: Hip-Hop Wax Facts, Straight From the Original Artists*. Somerville, MA: Wax Facts Press.

Coleman, Brian. (2007). *Check the Technique: Liner Notes for Hip-Hop Junkies*. New York: Villard.

Coleman, Brian. (2014). *Check the Technique, Volume 2: Liner Notes for Hip-Hop Junkies*. Somerville, MA: Wax Facts Press.

Coleman, Gabriella (2015) *Hacker, Hoaxer, Whistleblower, Spy: The Many Faces of Anonymous*. New York: Verso.

Collins, Nicolas. (2004). *Hardware Hacking*. Chicago: Nicolas Collins.

Collins, Timothy. (2017). Wu-Tang Clan versus Jean Baudrillard: Rap Poetics and Simulation. *The Journal of Popular Culture*, Vol. 50, No. 2 pp. 1-21.

Conner, Thomas. (2012, October 18). Jail Time Might Not Hurt Sales. *Chicago Sun-Times*, p. 4.

Conner, Thomas. (2012, October 20). Rappers' Beefs Sizzle on Social Media. *Chicago Sun-Times*, p. 3.

Cooper, Martha. (2004). *Hip-Hop Files: Photographs, 1979-1984*. Berlin: From Here to Fame Publishing.

Corbett, John. (1994). *Extended Play: Sounding Off from John Cage to Dr. Funkenstein*. Durham, NC: Duke University Press.

Coscarelli, Joe. (2015, July 26). Hologram Performance by Chief Keef Is Shut Down by Police. *New York Times*. Retrieved on July 8, 2018 from https://www.nytimes.com/2015/07/27/arts/music/hologram-performance-by-chief-keef-is-shut-down-by-police.html?smid=tw-nytimes&_r=0

Cronenberg, David. (1983). *Videodrome*. Directed by David Cronenberg. Los Angeles: Universal Pictures.

Cruz, Décio Torres. (2014). *Postmodern Metanarratives: Blade Runner and Literature in the Age of Image*. New York: Palgrave Macmillan.

Csicsery-Ronay, Jr., Istvan. (1992). Futuristc Flu, or, The Revenge of the Future. In, George Slusser & Tom Shippey (Eds.), *Fiction 2000: Cyberpunk and the Future of Narrative*, pp. 26-45.

dälek. (2007). "(Subversive Script)." On *Abandoned Language* [LP]. Los Angeles: Ipecac Records.

Davenport-Hines, Richard. (1998). *Gothic: Four Hundred Years of Excess, Horror, Evil and Ruin*. New York: North Point Press.

Davis, Erik. (1998). *TechGnosis: Myth, Magic, and Mysticism in the Age of Information*. New York: Harmony Books.

de Certeau, Michel. (1984). *The Practice of Everyday Life*. Berkeley, CA: University of California Press.

de Lauzirika, Charles. (2007). *Dangerous Days: The Making of Blade Runner*. [DVD]. Directed by Charles de Lauzirika. Los Angeles: Warner Home Video.

deAK, Edit. (1983, May). Culture is the Most Fertilized Substance. *Artforum*. pp. 88-93.

Deeley, Michael. (2008). *Blade Runners, Deer Hunters & Blowing the Bloody Doors Off: My Life in Cult Movies*. London: Faber & Faber.

Def, Mos & Kweli, Talib. (1998) "Respiration" (featuring Common) [Black Star] from *Mos Def & Talib Kweli are Black Star*. New York: Rawkus Records.

DeLanda, Manuel. (1997). *A Thousand Years of Nonlinear History*. New York: Zone Books.

Delany, Samuel R. (1966). *Empire Star*. New York: Ace Books.

Delany, Samuel R. (1975). *Dhalgren*. New York: Ace Books.

Demers, Joanna. (2006). *Steal This Music: How Intellectual Property Law Affects Musical Creativity*. Athens, GA: University of Georgia Press.

Dennett, Daniel. (1998). *Brainchildren: Essays on Designing Minds,* MIT Press.

Derrida, Jacques. (1994). *Specters of Marx*. New York: Routledge.

Derrida, Jacques. (1996). *Archive Fever: A Freudian Impression*. Chicago: University of Chicago Press.

Dery, Mark (Ed.). (1993, Fall). Flame Wars: The Discourse of Cyberculture. *The South Atlantic Quarterly*, Vol 92, No. 4.

Dery, Mark. (1994). *Flame Wars: The Discourse of Cyberculture*. Durham, MC: Duke University Press.

Dery, Mark. (1996a). *Escape Velocity: Cyberculture at the End of the Century*. New York: Grove Press.

Dery, Mark. (1996b) Downsizing the Future. Beyond *Blade Runner* with Mike Davis. Retrieved March 17, 2016 from http://www.thing.net/~rdom/ucsd/DavisFuture.pdf

Dery, Mark. (2007). Wired Man's Burden: The Incredible Whiteness of Being Digital. In Anna Everett and Amber J. Wallace (Eds.), *AfroGeeks: Beyond the Digital Divide*. Santa Barbara, CA: Center for Black Studies Research, pp. 29-48.

Dery, Mark. (2016, February 1). Black to the Future: Afrofuturism (3.0). *Die Fabrikzeitung*. Retrieved March 17, 2017 from http://www.fabrikzeitung.ch/black-to-the-future-afrofuturism-3-0/

Desser, David. (1991). Race, Space and Class: The Politics of the SF Film from *Metropolis* to *Blade Runner*. In Judith B. Kerman (Ed.), *Retrofitting Blade Runner*. Madison, WI: University of Wisconsin Press, pp. 110-123.

Dettmar, Kevin H. & Richey, William. (1999). *Reading Rock and Roll: Authenticity, Appropriation, Aesthetics*. New York: Columbia University Press.

Doctorow, Cory. William Gibson Interview Transcript, 1999. In, Patrick A. Smith (Ed.), *Conversations with William Gibson*. Jackson, MS: University Press of Mississippi, 2014. pp. 152-168.

Dot, The Black. (2005). *Hip-Hop Decoded: From Its Ancient Origins to Its Modern-Day Matrix*. New York: MOME Publishing.

Draaisma, Douwe. (2000). *Metaphors of Memory: A History of Ideas about the Mind*. Cambridge: Cambridge University Press.

Drake, David. (2014, March 13). Not a Biter I'm a Writer? The Phenomenon of Swagger Jacking. *Complex*. Retrieved February 4, 2016, from http://www.complex.com/music/2014/03/not-a-biter-im-a-writer

Du Bois, W. E. B. (1903). *The Souls of Black Folk*, Chicago: A.C. McClurg & Co.

Durgnat, Raymond. (1971). *Films and Feelings*. Cambridge, MA: MIT Press.

Eagle, Open Mike. (2017). "95 Radios" (featuring Has-Lo). On *Brick Body Kids Still Daydream* [LP]. Tucson, AZ: Mello Music Group.

Edwards, Elisa. (2011). *Race, Aliens, and the U.S Government in African American Science Fiction*. London: LIT Verlag.

Edwards, Paul. (2009). *How to Rap: The Art and Science of the Hip-Hop MC*. Chicago: Chicago Review Press.

Edwards, Paul. (2013). *How to Rap 2: Advanced Flow & Delivery Techniques*. Chicago: Chicago Review Press.

Edwards, Paul. (2015). *The Concise Guide to Hip-Hop Music: A Fresh Look at the Art of Hip-hop, from Old-School Beats to Freestyle Rap*. New York: St. Martin's Griffin.

Eglash, Ron. (1995). African Influences in Cybernetics. In Chris Hables Gray (Ed.), *The Cyborg Handbook*. New York: Routledge. pp. 17-27.

*Ego Trip*. (2012, March 27) Rammellzee on the Making of "Beat Bop" (previously unpublished interview, 1999). *Egotripland*. Retrieved on May 5, 2017 from http://www.egotripland.com/rammellzee-beat-bop/

Eisenstein, Jacob, O'Connor, Brendan, Smith, Noah A., & Xing, Eric P. (2012, October 23). Mapping the Geographical Diffusion of New Words. Retrieved November 24, 2012 from http://arxiv.org/abs/1210.5268

Empson, William. (1947). *7 Types of Ambiguity*. New York: New Directions.

Ernst, Wolfgang. (2013). *Digital Memory and the Archive*. Minneapolis, MN: University of Minnesota Press.

Erwin, J., Malcolm, S. A., Duncan-Mao, A., Matthews, A., Monroe, J., Samuel, A., & Satten, Vanessa. (2006, August). "Told You So: The Making of Reasonable Doubt." *XXL Magazine*, 10, 7. pp. 89-102.

Eshun, Kodwo. (1998). *More Brilliant Than the Sun: Adventures in Sonic Fiction*. London: Quartet.

Eshun, Kodwo. (2003, Summer). Further Considerations on Afrofuturism. *The New Centennial Review*, Vol. 3, No. 2, pp. 287-302

Eshun, Kodwo. (2013). Stealing One's Own Corpse: Afrofuturism as Speculative Heresy. In, Keith, Naima J. & Whitley, Zoé (Eds). *The Shadows Took Shape*. New York: The Studio Museum in Harlem. pp. 117-120.

Eshun, Kodwo. (in-press). The Co-Evolution of Technology and Humanity: An Interview with William Gibson (November, 1996). In Roy Christopher (Ed.), *Follow for Now, Volume 2: More Interviews with Friends and Heroes*. Brooklyn, NY: Punctum Books.

Eshun, Kodwo & Sagar, Anjalika (Eds.). (2007). *The Ghosts of Songs: The Film Art of the Black Audio Film Collective*. Liverpool: Liverpool University Press.

Evans, Claire. (2012). It Turned into Birds. *Vice Magazine*. Retrieved March 17, 2012 from http://motherboard.vice.com/blog/it-evolved-into-birds-ten-science-fictional-thinkers-on-the-past-and-future-of-cyberpunk

Fairclough, Norman. (1992). *Discourse and Social Change*. Cambridge: Polity.

Fancher, Hampton & Peoples, David. (1982). *Blade Runner*. [Motion picture]. Directed by Ridley Scott. Los Angeles: The Ladd Company/Warner Bros.

Fanon, Frantz. (1963). *The Wretched of the Earth*. New York: Grove Weidenfeld.

Fanon, Frantz. (1967). *Black Skin, White Masks*. New York: Grove.

Feld, Steven (1994). Aesthetics of Iconicity of Style, or "Lift-Up-Over Sounding": Getting into the Kaluli Groove. In, Charles Keli & Steven Feld (Eds.), *Music Grooves: Essays and Dialogues*. Chicago: University of Chicago Press. pp. 109-150.

Fernandes, Sujatha. (2011). *Close to the Edge: In Search of the Global Hip-Hop Generation*. New York: Verso.

Fernandez, Manny. (2007, October 5). When Presidents Visited the South Bronx. City Room Blog, *The New York Times*. Retrieved January 17, 2017 from https://cityroom.blogs.nytimes.com/2007/10/05/when-presidents-visited-the-south-bronx/

Fernando, Jr., S.H. (1994). *The New Beats: Exploring the Music, Culture, and Attitudes of Hip-Hop*. New York: Anchor Books.

Finn, Christine A. (2001). *Artifacts: An Archeologists Year in Silicon Valley*. Cambridge, MA: MIT Press.

Fisher, Mark (2009, December 10). The Age of Consent. *New Statesman*. Retrieved April 23, 2018 from https://www.newstatesman.com/television/2009/12/business-culture-cultural

Fisher, Mark. (2014). *Ghosts of My Life: Writings on Depression, Hauntology, and Lost Futures*. London, UK: Zer0 Books.

Fiske, John. (1987). *Television Culture*. New York: Routledge.

Flash, Grandmaster. (2008). *The Adventures of Grandmaster Flash: My Life, My Beats*. New York: Broadway.

Foster, Hal. (1985). *Recodings: Art, Spectacle, Cultural Politics*. Seattle, WA: Bay Press.

Foster, Hal. (2004, Fall). An Archival Impulse. *October*, 110. pp. 3–22.

Flür, Wolfgang. (2000). *Kraftwerk: I Was a Robot*. London: Sanctuary.

Foucault, Michel. (1997). *Discipline and Punish: The Birth of the Prison*. New York: Pantheon.

Franz, Barbara. (2015). *Immigrant Youth, Hip- Hop, and Online Games: Alternative Approaches to the Inclusion of Working-Class and Second Generation Migrant Teens*. Lanham, MD: Lexington Books.

Freddy, Fab 5. (2011). Rammellzee. In Jeffrey Deitch, Roger Gastman, and Aaron Rose (Eds.), *Art in the Streets*. New York: Skira Rizzoli Publications. pp. 90-95.

Fricke, Jim & Ahearn, Charlie. (2002). *Yes Yes, Y'all: Oral History of Hip-Hop's First Decade*. New York: Da Capo.

Fusco, Katherine. (2015). Voices from Beyond the Grave: Virtual Tupac's Live Performance at Coachella. *Camera Obscura* 89, Vol. 30, No. 2, pp. 28-53.

Gaines, Donna. (1994). Border Crossing in the U.S.A. In Andrew Ross & Tricia Rose (Eds.), *Microphone Fiends: Youth Music & Youth Culture*. New York: Routledge, pp. 227-234).

Galli, Chuck. (2009). Hip-Hop Futurism: Remixing Afrofuturism and the Hermeneutics of Identity. *Honors Projects Overview*, Paper 18. Retrieved December 15, 2016 from https://digitalcommons.ric.edu/honors_projects/18/

Gardner, Martin. (2001). *Did Adam and Eve Have Navels?* W. W. Norton & Company.

Gates, Henry Louis, Jr. (1988). *The Signifying Monkey: A Theory of African-American Literary Criticism*. New York: Oxford University Press.

Gates, Henry Louis, Jr. (2010). Foreword. In Adam Bradley and Andrew DuBois (Eds.), *The Anthology of Rap*. New Haven, CT: Yale University Press. pp. xxii-xxvii.

Genosko, Gary, 2012. *Remodelling Communication: From WWII to the WWW*. Toronto: University of Toronto Press.

George, Nelson. (1994). *Buppies, B-Boys, Baps & Bohos: Notes on Post-Soul Black Culture*. New York: HarperCollins.

George, Nelson. (2002). Introduction: The Will to Joy. In Fricke & Ahearn (Eds.), *Yes Yes, Y'all: Oral History of Hip-Hop's First Decade*. New York: Da Capo.

George, Nelson (2004). Hip-Hop's Founding Fathers Speak the Truth. In Murray Foreman and Mark Anthony Neal (Eds.). *That's the Joint! The Hip-Hop Studies Reader*. New York: Routledge. pp. 45-60.

Gibbs, Jr., Raymond W. (1994). *The Poetics of Mind: Figurative Thought, Language, and Understanding*. Cambridge: Cambridge University Press.

Gibson, William. (1995). *Johnny Mnemonic* [screenplay]. New York: Ace Books.

Gibson, William. (2002, November 6). Since 1948. Retrieved on July 17, 2018 from http://williamgibsonbooks.com/source/source.asp

Gibson, William. (2003). *Pattern Recognition*. New York: Putnam.

Gibson, William. (2005, July). God's Little Toys. *WIRED*, 13.7.

Gibson, William. (2012). *Distrust That Particular Flavor*. New York: Putnam.

Gifford, Barry. (1990). *Wild at Heart: The Story of Sailor and Lula*. New York: Grove Weidenfeld.

Giles, Jim. (2012, November 17). Twitter Shows Language Evolves in Cities. *New Scientist*, 2891.

Gill, Ed. (2014). MC Rammellzee Interview: June, 1995. In James Lavelle (Ed.), *Urban Archaeology: Twenty-One Years of MoWax*. New York: Rizzoli.

Gillespie, Blake (2017, April 27). How the Antipop Consortium Dragged Rap into the Millennium. *Bandcamp Daily*. Retrieved May 30, 2017 from https://daily.bandcamp.com/2017/04/27/antipop-consortium-feature/

Gilmore, Ruth Wilson, Race and Globalization, In Ronald Johnn Johnson, Peter James Taylor, and Michael Watts (Eds.), *Geographies of Global Change: Remapping the World*. Malden, MA: Wiley-Blackwell, 2002. pp. 261-274.

Gilroy, Paul. (1985, February 5). Rap the Rhyme. *New Internationalist*.

Gilroy, Paul. (1993). *The Black Atlantic: Modernity and Double Consciousness*. Cambridge, MA: Harvard University Press.

Gilroy, Paul. (2001). *Against Race: Imagining Political Culture Beyond the Color Line*. Cambridge, MA: Belknap Press.

Gilroy, Paul. (2010). *Darker than Blue: On the Moral Economies of Black Atlantic Culture*. Cambridge: Harvard University Press.

Gitlin, Todd. (2001). *Media Unlimited: How the Torrent of Images and Sounds Overwhelms Our Lives*. New York: Metropolitan Books.

Gledhill, Evan Hayles. (2017). The Posthuman Monstrous Can Only Be Gothic, or Screening Alien Sex Fiends. In, Anya Heise-von der Lippe (Ed.), *Posthuman Gothic*. Cardiff, UK: University of Wales Press. pp. 215-230.

Gleick, James. (2008, January 6). Keeping It Real. *The New York Times Magazine*. Retrieved March 17, 2016 from https://www.nytimes.com/2008/01/06/magazine/06wwln-lede-t.html

Goldberg, David Albert Mhadi. (2004). The Scratch is Hip-hop: Appropriating the Phonographic Medium. In Ron Eglash, Jennifer L. Croissant, Giovanna Di Charro & Rayvon Fouche (Eds.), *Appropriating Technology: Vernacular Science and Social Power*. Saint Paul: University of Minnesota Press. pp. 107-144.

Goodman, Steve. (2010). *Sonic Warfare: Sound, Affect, and the Ecology of Fear*. Cambridge, MA: MIT Press.

Gordon, Avery F. (1997). *Ghostly Matters: Haunting and the Sociological Imagination*. Minneapolis, MN: University of Minnesota Press.

Greaney, Patrick. (2014). *Quotational Practices: Repeating the Future in Contemporary Art*. Minneapolis, MN: University of Minnesota Press.

Greelish, David. (2013, April 2). An Interview with Computing Pioneer Alan Kay. *Time*. Retrieved June 14, 2018 from http://techland.time.com/2013/04/02/an-interview-with-computing-pioneer-alan-kay/

Green, Renée. (2003). Affection Afflictions: My Alien/My Self or More "Reading at Work." In Greg Tate (Ed.), *Everything But the Burden: What White People are Taking From Black Culture*. New York: Harlem Moon/Broadway. pp. 227-243.

Greenberg, Andy. (2012). *This Machine Kills Secrets*. New York: Dutton Adult.

Guffey, Robert. (2015). *Chameleo: A Strange but True Story of Invisible Spies, Heroin Addiction, and Homeland Security*. New York: O/R Books.

Gwinn, Mary Ann. (2014). Futuristic Fantasy Lives Now for Author William Gibson, 2007. In, Patrick A. Smith (Ed.), *Conversations with William Gibson*. Jackson, MS: University Press of Mississippi. pp. 178-182.

Hafner, Katie & Markoff, John. (1991). *Cyberpunk: Outlaws and Hackers on the Computer Frontier*. New York: Touchstone.

Hagerty, Neil & Herrema, Jennifer. (1990). *Twin Infinitives* [LP]. Recorded by Royal Trux. Chicago: Drag City.

Haj-Najafu, Daryoush. (2010, July 5). Rammellzee: Fashion for an Exploding, Dance-Making Brain. *Vice*. Retrieved March 11, 2018 from https://www.vice.com/en_uk/article/3bemx8/rammellzee-fashion

hampton, dream. (1994, November). Kiss Yourself Goodbye: A New Refutation of the Alternative Nigga. *Village Voice*. Retrieved March 7, 2018 from http://dreamhampton.com/kiss-yourself

hampton, dream. (1998, December). Oh Gods. *Village Voice*. Retrieved March 7, 2018 from http://dreamhampton.com/rza

hampton, dream. (2006, February). Octavia E. Butler, Science Fiction Visionary. *Village Voice*. Retrieved March 7, 2018 from http://dreamhampton.com/octavia

Harkness, Geoff. (2014). *Chicago Hustle & Flow: Gangs, Gangsta Rap, and Social Class*. Minneapolis, MN: University of Minnesota Press.

Hauer, Rutger. (2007). *All Those Moments: Stories of Heroes, Villains, Replicants, and Blade Runners* (with Patrick Quinlan). New York: HarperCollins.

Hayles, N. Katherine. (1999). *How We Became Posthuman: Virtual Bodies in Cybernetics, Literature, and Informatics*. Chicago: University of Chicago Press.

Heartney, Eleanor. (1985, March). Appropriation and the Loss of Authenticity. *New Art Examiner*. pp. 26-30.

Heath, Ashley. (1997, April). Jesus is a Soul Man. *Face*.

Hebdige, Dick. (1979). *Subculture: The Meaning of Style*. New York: Routledge.

Heller, Jason. (2018). *Strange Stars: David Bowie, Pop Music, and the Decade Sci-Fi Exploded*. Brooklyn, NY: Melville Hous.

Henthorne, Tom. (2011). *William Gibson: A Literary Companion*. Jefferson, NC: McFarland & Co.

Hess, Mickey. (2006). Was Foucault a Plagiarist? Hip-hop Sampling and Academic Citation. *Computers and Composition*, 23, pp. 280-295.

Hess, Mickey. (2007). *Is Hip-Hop Dead? The Past, Present, and Future of America's Most Wanted Music*. Westport, CT: Praeger.

Hess, Mickey. (2012). The Rap Career. In Murray Forman and Mark Anthony Neal (Eds.), *That's the Joint: The Hip-hop Studies Reader*. New York: Routledge.

Heuser, Sabine. (2003). *Virtual Geographies: Cyberpunk at the Intersection of the Postmodern and Science Fiction*. Amsterdam: Rodolphi.

Hinds, Selwun Seyfu. (2002). *Gunshots in My Cook-Up: Bits and Bites from a Hip-Hop Caribbean Life*. New York: Atria.

Hirsch, Marianne & Smith, Valerie. (2002, Autumn) Feminism and Cultural Memory: An Introduction. *Signs*, Vol. 28, No. 1, pp. 1-19.

Hogle, Jerrod E. (Ed.). (2002). *The Cambridge Companion to Gothic Fiction*. Cambridge, UK: Cambridge University Press.

Honda, DJ. (1998). "Travelin' Man" (featuring Mos Def). from *hII* [album]. Sony.

Howard, David, N. (2004). *Sonic Alchemy: Visionary Music Producers and Their Maverick Recordings*. Milwaukee, MI: Hal Leonard.

Huhtamo, Erkki. (2013). *Illusions in Motion: Media Archeology of the Moving Panorama and Related Spectacles*. Cambridge, MA: MIT Press.

Hutcheon, Linda. (1985). *A Theory of Parody: The Teachings of Twentieth-Century Art Forms*. New York: Methuen.

Hutcheon, Linda. (2006). *A Theory of Adaptation*. New York: Routledge.

Huyseen, Andreas. (2003). *Present Pasts: Urban Palimpsests and the Politics of Memory*. Stanford, CA: Stanford University Press.

Ice-T. (1987). "Rhyme Pays." On *Rhyme Pays* [LP]. New York: Sire/Warner Bros.

Jacobson, Karen (Ed.). (2013). *Radical Presence: Black Performance in Contemporary Art*. Houston, TX: Contemporary Arts Museum Houston.

Jakobson, Roman. (1960). Concluding Statement: Linguistics and Poetics. In Thomas Albert Sebeok (Ed.), *Style in Language*. Cambridge: MIT Press.

James, Jamillah. (2013). RAMM: ▨LL:Z▨▨. In, Keith, Naima J. & Whitley, Zoé (Eds). *The Shadows Took Shape*. New York: The Studio Museum in Harlem, pp. 36-37.

Jay-Z. (2001). "Takeover." On *The Blueprint* [LP]. New York: Roc-A-Fella/Def Jam.

Jay-Z. (2005). "Diamonds from Sierra Leone" (Remix) [Kanye West featuring Jay-Z]. On *Late Registration* [LP]. New York: Roc-A-Fella/Def Jam.

Jay-Z (with dream hampton). (2010). *Decoded*. New York: Spiegel & Grau.

Jenkins, Henry. (1992). *Textual Poachers: Television Fans & Participatory Culture*. New York: Routledge.

Jenkins, Henry. (2006). *Convergence Culture: Where Old and New Media Collide*. New York: New York University Press.

Jennings, Humphrey. (1985). *Pandaemonium, 1660-1886: The Coming of the Machine as Seen by Contemporary Observers*. London: Icon Books.

Jones, David J. (2011). *Gothic Machine: Textualities, Pre-cinematic Media and Film in Popular Visual Culture, 1670-1910*, University of Wales Press.

Jones, Grace. (2015). *I'll Never Write My Memoirs*. New York: Gallery Books.

Jones, Thomas. (2011, September 22). William Gibson: Beyond Cyberspace. *The Guardian*. Retrieved December 14, 2011 from http://www.guardian.co.uk/books/2011/sep/22/william-gibson-beyond-cyberspace

Josiffe, Chris. (2018, February). A Little History of Spirit Technology. *Fortean Times*. pp. 30-37.

Jünger, Ernst. (1992). *Aladdin's Problem*. New York: Marsilio Publishers Corp.

Kahn, Ashley. (2006). *The House That Trane Built: The Story of Impulse Records*. New York: W.W. Norton & Co.

Kangas, Chaz. (2013, November 5). The History of Horrorcore Rap. *LA Weekly*.

Kanin, Garson. (1954). *It Should Happen to You*. Directed by George Cukor. Hollywood, CA: Columbia Pictures.

Kass, Ras. (2001). "Van Gogh" from *Van Gogh* [Promo CD]. Priority Records.

Katz, Mark. (2004). *Capturing Sound: How Technology has Changed Music*. Berkeley, CA: University of California Press.

Katz, Mark. (2012). *Groove Music: The Art and Culture of the Hip-hop DJ*. New York: Oxford University Press.

Keith, Naima J. & Whitley, Zoé. (2013). *The Shadows Took Shape*. New York: The Studio Museum in Harlem.

Kehinde, Owoeye Durojaiye. (2011). *Intertextuality and the Novels of Amos Tutuola and Ben Okri*. Saarbrücken, Deutschland: Lambert Academic Publishing.

Kelley, Mike. (1985). Urban Gothic, *Spectacle*, no. 3.

Kelly, James Patrick, & Kessel, John. (2007). *Rewired: The Post-Cyberpunk Anthology*. San Francisco: Tachyon.

Kennedy, Randy. (2010, July 2). Rammellzee, Hip-Hop and Graffiti Pioneer, Dies at 49. *The New York Times*. Retrieved March 11, 2018 from http://www.nytimes.com/2010/07/02/arts/02rammellzee.html

Kerman, Judith B. (Ed.). (1991). *Retrofitting Blade Runner*. Madison, WI: University of Wisconsin Press.

Khabeer, Su'ad Abdul. (2016). *Muslim Cool: Race, Religion, and Hip-Hop in the United States*. New York: New York University Press.

Khair, Tabish. (2009). *The Gothic, Postcolonialism, and Otherness: Ghosts from Elsewhere*. New York: Palgrave Macmillan, 2009.

Klein, Norman M. (1997). *The History of Forgetting: Los Angeles and the Erasure of Memory*. New York: Verso.

Klein, Norman, M. (2004). *The Vatican to Vegas: A History of Special Effects*, New York, The New Press.

Kleinberg, Ethan. (2017). *Haunting History: For a Deconstructive Approach to the Past*. Stanford, CA: Stanford University Press.

Knight, Michael Muhammed. (2007). *The Five Percenters: Islam, Hip-Hop and the Gods of New York*. Oxford, UK: Oneworld.

Kövecses, Zoltán. (2000). *Metaphor and Emotion: Language, Culture, and Body in Human Feeling*. Cambridge: Cambridge University Press.

Krims, Adam. (2000). *Rap Music and the Poetics of Identity*. Cambridge: Cambridge University Press.

KRS-One. (1995). "Out for Fame." On *KRS-One* [LP]. New York: Jive.

Krzeczowski, Jake. (2018). Why is the Chicago Police Department Targeting Chief Keef? In Javon Johnson & Kevin Coval (Eds.), *The End of Chiraq: A Literary Mixtape*. Evanston, IL: Northwestern University Press, pp. 68-72.

Kugelberg, Johan. (Ed.). (2015). *Renegades of Rhythm: DJ Shadow & Cut Chemist Play Afrika Bambaataa*. New York: Boo-Hooray.

Kuhn, Thomas. (1977). *The Essential Tension: Selected Studies in Scientific Tradition and Change*. Chicago: University of Chicago Press.

Lacasse, Serge. (2000). Intertextuality and Hypertextuality in Recorded Popular Music. In Michael Talbot (Ed.), *The Musical Work: Reality or Invention?* Liverpool: Liverpool University Press. pp. 35-58.

Lacitis, Erik. (2017, June 24). "Flying saucers" Became a Thing 70 Years Ago Saturday with Sighting Near Mount Rainier. *Seattle Times*. Retrieved June 24, 2017 from https://www.seattletimes.com/seattle-news/northwest/flying-saucers-became-a-thing-70-years-ago-saturday-with-sighting-near-mount-rainier/

Ladd, Michael C. (2003). The New Mythology Began Without Me. In Greg Tate (Ed.), *Everything But the Burden: What White People are Taking from Black Culture*. New York: Harlem Moon, pp. 106-109.

Lakoff, George & Johnson, Mark. (1980). *Metaphors We Live By*. Chicago: University of Chicago Press.

Landsberg, Alison. (1995). Prosthetic Memory: Total Recall and Blade Runner. In Mike Featherstone & Roger Burrows (Eds.), *Cyberspace/Cyberbodies/Cyberpunk: Cultures of Technological Embodiment*. New York: Sage. pp. 175-189.

Landsburg, Alan & Sally. (1974). *In Search of Ancient Mysteries*. New York: Bantam.

Lasn, Kalle. (1999). *Culture Jam: The Uncooling of America*. New York: William Morrow.

Lanois, Daniel. (2010). *Soul Mining: A Musical Life*. London: Faber & Faber.

Lavender, Isiah III. (2015). Delany Encounters, Or Another Reason Why I Study Race and Racism in Science Fiction. In Nisi Shawl & Bill Campbell (Eds.), *Stories for Chip: A Tribute to Samuel R. Delany*. Greenbelt, MD: Rosarium Publishing. pp. 38-50.

Leppihalme, Ritva. (1997). *Culture Bumps: An Empirical Approach to the Translation of Allusions*. Bristol, PA: Multilingual Matters.

Lepselter, Susan. (2016). *The Resonance of Unseen Things: Poetics, Power, Captivity, and UFOs in the American Uncanny*. Ann Arbor, MI: University of Michigan Press.

Levy, Steven. (1984). *Hackers: Heroes of the Computer Revolution*. New York: Anchor Press/Doubleday.

Lievrouw, Leah A. (2011). *Alternative and Activist New Media*. Cambridge, UK: Polity.

Lipari, Lisbeth. (2013). Hansberry's Hidden Transcript. *The Journal of Popular Culture*, Vol 46, No. 1, pp. 119-142.

Lock, Graham. (1989). *Forces in Motion: The Music and Thoughts of Anthony Braxton*. New York: Da Capo.

Lock, Graham. (1999). *Blutopia: Visions of the future and Revisions of the Past in the Work of Sun Ra, Duke Ellington, and Anthony Braxton*. Durham, NC: Duke University Press.

Long, Marion. (2007, August). Q&A: William Gibson: Are You Spooked Yet? *Discover*. pp. 68-69.

Lordz of Brooklyn. (1995). "Tales from the Rails" (featuring Rammellzee). On *All in the Family*. [LP]. Los Angeles: American Recordings.

Lovink, Geert. (2002a). *Dark Fiber: Tracking Critical Internet Culture*. Cambridge, MA: MIT Press.

Lovink, Geert. (2002b). *Uncanny Networks: Dialogues with the Virtual Intelligentsia*. Cambridge, MA: MIT Press.

Luker, Ralph E. (2003, Summer). Quoting, Merging, and Sampling the Dream: Martin Luther King and Vernon Johns. *Southern Cultures*. pp. 28-48.

Lynch, David & Gifford, Barry. (1990). *Wild at Heart* [Motion picture]. Los Angeles: PolyGram Filmed Entertainment.

Magnus, Kathy Dow. (2006, Spring). The Unaccountable Subject: Judith Butler and the Social Conditions of Intersubjective Agency. *Hypatia* vol. 21, no.2.

Maher, George Ciccariello. (2005). Brechtian Hip-Hop: Didactics and Self-Production in Post-Gangsta Political Mixtapes. *Journal of Black Studies, 36*(1), pp. 129-160.

Marcus, Greil. (1989). *Lipstick Traces: A Secret History of the Twentieth Century.* Cambridge, MA: Harvard University Press.

Masri, Heather. (2008). *Science Fiction: Stories and Contexts.* New York: Bedford/St. Martin's.

Matos, Michaelangelo. (2011, September 28). The Shove Felt Round the World: The Historical Significance of That Time KRS-One Bum-Rushed a P.M. Dawn Show and Shoved Prince Be Offstage. *The Stranger*. Retrieved May 2, 2018 from https://www.thestranger.com/seattle/the-shove-felt-round-the-world/Content?oid=10126832

McCaffery, Larry (Ed.). (1991). *Storming the Reality Studio: A Casebook of Cyberpunk and Postmodern Fiction.* Durham, NC: Duke University Press.

McCormick, Carlo, Rammellzzee: Now, Voyager. *Art Net*. Retrieved March 17, 2017 from http://www.artnet.com/magazineus/features/mccormick/rammellzee-4-10-12.asp

McGlone, Matthew S. (2005a). Contextonomy: The Art of Quoting Out of Context. *Media, Culture & Society*, Vol 27(4), pp. 511-522.

McGlone, Matthew S. (2005b, June). Quoted Out of Context: Contextonomy and Its Consequences. *Journal of Communication*, pp. 330-346.

McGlone, Matthew S. & Tofighbakhsh, Jessica. (2000, September). Birds of a Feather Flock Conjointly (?): Rhyme as Reason in Aphorisms. *Psychological Science*, Vol. 11 No. 5, pp. 424-428.

McLeod, Kembrew. (2002). The Politics and History of Hip-hop Journalism. In Steve Jones (Ed.), *Pop Music and the Press*. Philadelphia, PA: Temple University Press, pp. 156-167.

McLeod, Kembrew. (2011). How Copyright Law Changed Hip-Hop: An Interview with Public Enemy's Chuck D and Hank Shocklee. In Kembrew McLeod & Rudolph Kuenzli (Eds.), *Cutting Across Media: Appropriation Art, Interventionist Collage, and Copyright Law*, pp. 152-157.

McLeod, Kembrew. (2005). *Freedom of Expression: Resistance and Repression in the Age of Intellectual Property*. Minneapolis, MN: University of Minnesota Press.

McLeod, Kembrew. (2015). An Oral History of Sampling: From Turntables to Mashups. In E. Navas, O. Gallagher, & x. burrough (Eds.), *The Routledge Companion to Remix Studies,* New York: Routledge, pp. 83-103.

McLeod, Kembrew & DiCola, Peter. (2011). *Creative License: The Law and Culture of Digital Sampling*. Durham, NC: Duke University Press. p. 55.

McLeod, Ken, (2003). Space Oddities: Aliens, Futurism and Meaning in Popular Music, in *Popular Music* 22, no. 3, pp. 337-355.

McLeod, Ken, (2016). Hip-Hop Holograms: Tupac Shakur, Technological Immortality, and Time Travel. In Reynaldo Anderson & Charles E. Jones (Eds.), *Afrofuturism 2.0: The Rise of Astro-Blackness*. Lanham: Lexington Books. pp. 109-124.

McLuhan, Marshall. (1951). *The Mechanical Bride*. New York: Vanguard Press.

McLuhan, Marshal. (1962). *The Gutenberg Galaxy: The Making of Typographic Man*. Toronto: University of Toronto Press.

McLuhan, Marshall. (1964). *Understanding Media: The Extensions of Man*. New York: McGraw-Hill.

McLuhan, Marshall. (1970). *Culture is Our Business*. New York: Ballantine Books.

McLuhan, Marshall & McLuhan, Eric (1988). *Laws of Media: The New Science*. Toronto, Canada: University of Toronto Press.

McLuhan, Marshall & Nevitt, Barrington. (1972). *Take Today: The Executive as Dropout*. New York: Harcourt Brace Jovanovich.

Metropolarity. (2016). *Style of Attack Report*. Philadelphia, PA: Metropolarity.

Miller, Ivor L. (2002). *Aerosol Kingdom: Subway Painters of New York City*. Jackson, MS: University Press of Mississippi.

Miller, Paul D. (2007). Bruce Sterling: Future Tense, 1999. In Roy Christopher (Ed.), *Follow for Now: Interviews with Friends and Heroes*. Seattle, WA: Well-Red Bear.

Minaj, Nicki. (2010). "Monster" [Kanye West featuring Jay-Z, Rick Ross, Nicki Minaj, and Bon Iver] from *My Beautiful Dark Twisted Fantasy* [LP]. New York: Roc-A-Fella/Def Jam.

Mishara, Aaron (2010). Klaus Conrad (1905–1961): Delusional Mood, Psychosis and Beginning Schizophrenia. *Schizophrenia Bulletin. 36* (1): pp. 9–13.

Mitnick, Kevin. (2011). *Ghost in the Wires: My Adventures as the World's Most Wanted Hacker*. New York: Back Bay Books.

Miyakawa, Felicia M. (2003). "The Duty of the Civilized is to Civilize the Uncivilized": Tropes of Black Nationalism in the Messages of Five Percent Rappers. In Ronald L. Jackson II & Elaine B. Richardson (Eds.), *Understanding African American Rhetoric: Classical Origins to Contemporary Innovations*. New York: Routledge. pp. 171-185.

Miyakawa, Felicia M. (2005). *Five Percenter Rap: God Hop's Music, Message, and Black Muslim Mission*. Bloomington, IN: Indiana University Press.

Monk, Patricia. *Alien Theory: The Alien Archetype in the Science Fiction Short Story*. Lanham, MD: Scarecrow Press.

Morgan, Tracy (with Anthony Bozza). (2009). *I Am the New Black*. New York, Spiegel & Grau.

Morrison, Toni. (1987). *Beloved: A Novel*. New York: Knopf.

Moten, Fred. (2003). *In the Break: The Aesthetics of the Black Radical Tradition*. Minneapolis, MN: University of Minnesota Press.

Moten, Fred. (2017). *Black and Blur: Consent Not to be a Single Being*. Durham, NC: Duke University Press.

Mudede, Charles. (2010). Twilight of the Goodtimes [unpublished lecture]. Retrieved September 22, 2016 from http://www.manifesta8.com/manifesta8. artist?nombre=&codigo=5 archived at https://web.archive. org/web/20120819084458/http://www.manifesta8.com/ manifesta8.artist?nombre=&codigo=5

Mungo, Paul & Clough, Bryan. (1992). *Approaching Zero: The Extraordinary Underworld of Hackers, Phreakers, Virus Writers, and Keyboard Criminals*. New York: Random House.

Myrie, Russell. (2008). *Don't Rhyme for the Sake of Riddlin': The Authorised Story of Public Enemy* . New York: Canongate.

Nas. (2001). "You're da Man." On *Stillmatic* [LP]. New York: Ill Will/Columbia.

Navas, Eduardo. (2012). *Remix Theory: The Aesthetics of Sampling*. New York: Springer.

Neale, Mark. (director). *William Gibson: No Maps for These Territories*. London: Docurama.

Neate, Patrick. (2003). *Where You're At: Notes from the Frontline of a Hip-Hop Planet*. London: Bloomsbury.

Nelson, Alondra. (2002, Summer). Future Texts. *Social Text*, 20(2), pp. 1-47.

Nichols, Preston B. & Moon, Peter. (1992). *The Montauk Project: Experiments in Time*. Westbury, NY: Sky Books.

Nichols, Preston B. & Moon, Peter. (1994). *Montauk Revisited: Adventures in Synchronicity*. Westbury, NY: Sky Books.

Nietzsche, Friedrich. (1974). *The Gay Science: With a Prelude in Rhymes and an Appendix of Songs*. New York: Vintage.

Ogg, Alex (with Upshall, David). (1999). *The Hip-Hop Years: A History of Rap*. London: Channel 4.

Ogg, Alex. (2002). *The Men Behind Def Jam: The Radical Rise of Russell Simmons and Rick Rubin*. London: Omnibus Press.

Olson, Parmy. (2012). *We Are Anonymous*. New York: Little, Brown, and Co.

Oworko, Lyle. (2011). *The Boombox Project: The Machines, the Music, and the Urban Underground*. New York: Abrams Image.

Orr, Mary. (2003). *Intertextuality: Debates and Contexts*. Cambridge, UK: Polity.

Parker, Alex, & Quinn, Michelle L. (2015, July 26). Chief Keef's Hologram Concert Shut Down by Police in Hammond. *Chicago Tribune*. Retrieved July 8, 2018 from http://www.chicagotribune.com/news/local/breaking/ct-chief-keef-hologram-concert-20150725-story.html

Pasco, A. H. (1994). *Allusion: A Literary Graft*. Toronto, Canada: University of Toronto Press.

Patke, Rajeev S. (2005). Benjamin on Art and Reproducibility: The Case of Music, in Andrew Benjamin (Ed.), *Walter Benjamin and Art*. New York: Continuum Books. pp. 185-208.

Patterson, Raymond R. (1969). *26 Ways of Looking at a Black Man*, New York: Award Books. p. 73.

Pepper, John Henry. (2006/1890). *The True History of Pepper's Ghost*. London: The Projection Box.

Perry, Imani. (2004). *Prophets of the Hood: Politics and Poetics in Hip-Hop*. Durham, NC: Duke University Press.

Perry, Imani. (2012). My Mic Sound Nice: Art, Community, and Consciousness. In Murray Forman & Mark Anthony Neal (Eds.), *That's the Joint! The Hip-hop Studies Reader*. New York: Routledge. pp. 504-517.

Petchauer, Emery. (2012). *Hip-Hop Culture in College Students' Lives: Elements, Embodiment, and Higher Education*. New York: Routledge.

Pettman, Dominic. (2006). *Love and Other Technologies: Retrofitting Eros for the Information Age*. New York: Fordham University Press.

Phase 2. (1996, February), Seeing Beyond the Vapors. *Rap Pages*, 5.1, p. 55.

Phillips, Rasheedah. (2014). *Recurrence Plot (and Other Time Travel Tales)*. Philadelphia, PA: Afro-Futurist Affair.

Phillips, Rasheedah. (2015). *Black Quantum Futurism: Theory & Practice*. Philadelphia, PA: Afro-Futurist Affair.

Phillips, Rasheedah. (2016). *Black Quantum Futurism: Space-Time Collapse I: From the Congo to the Carolinas*. Philadelphia, PA: Afro-Futurist Affair.

Phillips, Rasheedah. (2016). Future. In Kelly Fritsch, Claire O'Connor, & AK Thompson (Eds.), *Keywords for Radicals: The Contested Vocabulary of Late-Capitalist Struggle*. Chico, CA: AK Press. pp. 167-174.

Phillips, Rasheedah. (2017). *Telescoping Effect, Part One*. Philadelphia, PA: Afro-Futurist Affair.

Pink Floyd. (1968). *A Saucerful of Secrets* [LP]. London: EMI.

Piskor, Ed. (2014). *Hip-Hop Family Tree Book 2: 1981-1983*. Seattle, WA: Fantagraphics.

Porush, David. (1992). Frothing in the Synaptic Bath: What puts the Punk in Cyberpunk? In, George Slusser & Tom Shippey (Eds.), *Fiction 2000: Cyberpunk and the Future of Narrative*. pp. 246-261.

Poster, Mark. (1997). Cyberdemocracy: The Internet and the Public Sphere. In David Porter (Ed.), *Internet Culture*. New York: Routledge.

Powell, Arnett Kale & Olorunto, Adebayo Alabi. (2005). *The Hip-Hop Driven Life*. Baltimore, MD: Olorun/Afrikan World Books.

Pryor, Richard. (1976). *Bicentennial Nigger* [LP]. Burbank, CA: Warner Bros.

Public Enemy. (1988). *It Takes a Nation of Millions to Hold Us Back* [LP]. New York: Def Jam.

Punter, David. (1996). *The Literature of Terror, Volume 2: A History of Gothic Fictions from 1765 to the Present Day*. New York: Taylor & Francis.

Quinn, Chase. (2013, November 27). The Days of Future Past: Afrofuturism and Black Memory. *Hyperallergic*. Retrieved March 17, 2018 from https://hyperallergic.com/95760/the-days-of-future-past-afrofuturism-and-black-memory/

Ra, Sun. (2006). *Pathways to Unknown Worlds: El Saturn and Chicago's Afro-Futurist Underground 1954-68* (curated by John Corbett, Anthony Elms, and Terri Kapsalis). Chicago: White Walls.

Rakim (1987). "As the Rhyme Goes On" [Eric B. & Rakim]. On *Paid in Full* [LP]. New York: 4th & Broadway.

Rakim (1987). "I Know You Got Soul" [Eric B. & Rakim]. On *Paid in Full* [LP]. New York: 4th & Broadway.

Raley, Rita. (2009). *Tactical Media*. Minneapolis, MN: University of Minnesota Press.

Rammellzee (1979/2003). Iconic Treatise Gothic Futurism: Assassin Knowledges of the Remanipulated Square Points One to 720° to 1440°. http://www.gothicfuturism.com/rammellzee/01.html archived at https://web.archive.org/web/20130121193431/http://www.gothicfuturism.com/rammellzee/01.html

Rammellzee. (1986). *RAMM-ELL-ZEE*. Helmond, Holland: Gemeentemuseum Helmond.

Rammellzee. (1990). *Acts of Terrorism*. Kyoto, Japan: Kyoto Shoin International.

Rapatzikou, Tatiani G. (2004). *Gothic Motifs in the Fiction of William Gibson*. Amsterdam: Rodolphi.

Raudive, Konstantïns. (1971). *Breakthrough: An Amazing Experiment in Electronic Communication with the Dead*. New York: Taplinger.

Raush, Andrew J. (2011). *I Am Hip-Hop: Conversations on the Music and Culture*. Lanham, MD: Scarecrow Press.

Redmond, Sean. (2003). *Studying Blade Runner*. Leighton Buzzard, UK: Auteur.

Reynolds, Simon. (1995, June 24). Disco Infernal. *Melody Maker*.

Reynolds, Simon. (2000). The Nineties: The Best and the Worst. Retrieved on January 17, 2017 from http://members.aol.com/press101/90s.htm

Reynolds, Simon. (2011). *Retromania: Pop Culture's Addiction to Its Own Past*. New York: Faber & Faber.

Reynolds, Simon. (2012, October 5). You Are Not a Switch: Recreativity and the Modern Dismissal of Genius. *Slate*. http://www.slate.com/articles/arts/books/2012/10/against_recreativity_critics_and_artists_are_obsessed_with_remix_culture_.html

Reynolds, Simon (2013). *Generation Ecstasy: Into the World of Techno and Rave Culture*. New York: Routledge.

Ricoeur, Paul. *The Rule of Metaphor: Multidisciplinary Studies of the Creation of Meaning in Language*. Toronto: University of Toronto Press, 1977.

Ricoeur, Paul. *Memory, History, Forgetting*. Chicago: University of Chicago Press, 2004.

Riley, Boots. (2014). *Sorry to Bother You: A Screenplay*. San Francisco, CA: McSweeney's.

Riley, Boots. (2015). *Tell Homeland Security — We Are the Bomb*. Chicago: Haymarket Books.

Rogers, Everett M. *Diffusion of Innovations* 5th edition (New York: Free Press, 2003).

Rollefson, Griffith J. (2017). *Flip the Script: European Hip-Hop and the Politics of Postcoloniality*. Chicago: University of Chicago Press.

Ronda, James P. (1984). *Lewis & Clark Among the Indians*. University of Nebraska Press.

Roots, The. (2006). "False Media." On *Game Theory* [LP]. New York: Def Jam.

Rose, Marika. (2014, November, 18). The Uncomfortable Origins of "Afrofuturism". Retrieved March 16, 2015 from https://itself.blog/2014/11/18/the-uncomfortable-origins-of-afrofuturism/

Rose, Tricia. (1994). *Black Noise: Rap Music and Black Culture in Contemporary America*. Hanover, NH: Wesleyan University Press.

Rose, Tricia. (2008). *The Hip-Hop Wars: What We Talk About When We Talk About Hip-Hop — And Why It Matters*. New York: Basic Books.

Rosen, Miss. (2018, May 2). Remembering Rammellzee Through Stories of Those Who Knew Him. *Another Man Magazine*. Retrieved July 16, 2018 from http://www.anothermanmag.com/life-culture/10313/remembering-rammellzee-through-stories-of-those-who-knew-him

Rosenfeld R. & Messner, S. F. (1997). Markets, Morality, and an Institutional-Anomie Theory of Crime. In N. Passas & R. Agnew (Eds.), *The Future of Anomie Theory*. Boston: Northeastern University Press. pp. 207-224.

Roth-Gordon, J. (2009). Conversational sampling, race trafficking, and the invocation of the *gueto* in Brazilian hip hop. In H. S. Alim, A. Ibrahim & A, Pennycook (Eds.), *Global Linguistic Flows: Hip-hop Cultures, Youth Identities, and the Politics of Language*. New York: Routledge. pp. 63-77.

Rotman, Brian. (2008). *Becoming Beside Ourselves: The Alphabet, Ghosts, and Distributed Human Being*. Durham, NC: Duke University Press.

Roudiez, L. S. (1980). Introduction. In Julia Kristeva, *Desire in Language: A Semiotic Approach to Literature and Art*. New York: Columbia University Press. pp. 1-20.

Rowley, Stephen. (2005). False LA: *Blade Runner* and the Nightmare City. In Will Brooker (ed.), *The Blade Runner Experience*. pp. 203-212.

Rucker, Rudy. (1988). Report from Silicon Valley, *Science Fiction Eye* 1, no. 4.

Rucker, Rudy. (1999). *Seek! Selected Nonfiction*. New York: Four Walls Eight Windows.

Rucker, Rudy. (2015). *Nested Scrolls: The Autobiography of Rudolf von Bitter Rucker*. New York: Tor.

Russonello, Giovanni. (2015, April 30). Greg Tate on Burnt Sugar, Afrofuturism and Black Music's "Maroon Spaces". Retrieved on May 17, 2018 from http://www.capitalbop.com/greg-tate-on-burnt-sugar-afrofuturism-and-the-maroon-spaces-that-music-allows/

RZA. (2005). *The Wu-Tang Manual*. New York: Berkeley Publishing Group.

RZA. (2009). *The Tao of Wu*. New York: Riverhead.

Sammon, Paul M. (2017). *Future Noir: The Making of Blade Runner* (2nd Edition). New York: Dey St.

Sanders, Julie. (2006). *Adaptation and Appropriation: The New Critical Idiom*. New York: Routledge.

Savage, Steve. (2011). *Bytes and Backbeats: Repurposing Music in the Digital Age*. Ann Arbor: MI: University of Michigan Press.

Schloss, Joseph G. (2004). *Making Beats: The Art of Sample-Based Hip-hop*. Middletown, CT: Wesleyan University Press.

Schriber, Abbe. (2013). Sun Ra. In, Keith, Naima J. & Whitley, Zoé (Eds). *The Shadows Took Shape*. New York: The Studio Museum in Harlem. pp. 38-39.

Schultz, Kathryn. (2018, January 29). The Lost Giant of American Literature. *The New Yorker*.

Schwartz, Hillel. (1996). *The Culture of the Copy: Striking Likenesses, Unreasonable Facsimiles*. New York: Zone Books

Sconce, Jeffrey. (2000). *Haunted Media: Electronic Presence from Telegraphy to Television*. Durham, NC: Duke University Press.

Scott, James C. (1990). *Domination and the Arts of Resistance: Hidden Transcripts*. New Haven, CT: Yale University Press.

Scott-Heron, Gil. (1970). Whitey on the Moon. On *Small Talk at 125th and Lenox* [LP]. New York: Flying Dutchman.

Selzer, Michael. (1979). *Terrorist Chic: An Exploration of Violence in the Seventies*. New York: Hawthorn Books.

Shaffer, Tracy Stephenson & Gunn, Joshua, "'A Change is Gonna Come': On the Haunting of Music and Whiteness in Performance Studies," *Theatre Annual*, 59 (2006).

Sharpe, Christina. (2010). *Monstrous Intimacies: Making Post-Slavery Subjects*. Durham, NC: Duke University Press.

Sharpe, Christina. (2016). *In the Wake: On Blackness and Being*. Durham, NC: Duke University Press.

Shaviro, Steven. (2004). *Connected, or What it Means to Live in the Networked Society*. Minneapolis, MN: University of Minnesota Press.

Shaviro, Steven. (2010). *Post-Cinematic Affect*. London: Zer0 Books.

Shildrick, Margrit. (1996). Posthumanism and the Monstrous Body. *Body and Society* 2(1), pp. 1-15.

Shusterman, Richard. (2000). *Performing Live: Aesthetic Alternative for the Ends of Art*. Ithica, NY: Cornell University Press.

Sinker, Mark. (1992, February). Loving the Alien in Advance of the Landing. *The Wire*.

Smart, CK. A Turntable Experience: The Sonic World of Hop-Hop Turntablism. *SLAP Magazine*, pp. 74-75.

Smith, Abby. (1998, May/June). Preservation in the Future Tense. *CLIR Issues*, (3), 1, 6.

Smith, Danyel. (2000). Hit 'Em Up: On the Life and Death of Tupac Shakur. In Kevin Powell (Ed.), *Step into a World: A Global Anthology of the New Black Literature* . New York: John Wiley & Sons. pp. 133-140.

Smith, Sophy. (2013). *Hip-Hop Turntablism, Creativity, and Collaboration*. Burlington, VT: Ashgate.

Smitherman, Geneva. (1977). *Talkin and Testifyin: The Language of Black America*. New York: Houghton Mifflin.

Sonaike, Eva & Werner, Goetz. (2009). Ramm:ell:zee. In Sebastian Peiter (Ed.), *Guerilla Art*. London: Lawrence King Publishing. pp. 8-13.

Stanley, Thomas. (2014). *The Execution of Sun Ra, Vol. II.* Shelbyville, KY: Wasteland Press.

Steinberg, L. (1978). The Glorious Company (of Horse Thieves). In J. Lipman & R. Marshall (Eds.), *Art About Art*. New York: Dutton. pp. 21-32.

Steinskog, Erik. (2018). *Afrofuturism and Black Sound Studies.: Culture, Technology, and Things to Come*. London: Palgrave Macmillan.

Srephanou, Aspasia. (2017). Gothic Inhumanism: Promethianism, Nanotechnology, Accelerationism. In Anya Heise-von der Lippe (Ed.), *Posthuman Gothic*. Cardiff, UK: University of Wales Press. pp. 231-248.

Stephenson, Neal. (1996, December). Mother Earth, Mother Board. *WIRED*, 04.12.

Stephenson, Neal (2012). *Some Remarks: Essays and Other Writing*. New York: William Morrow.

Sterling, Bruce. (1986). Preface. In B. Sterling (Ed.), *Mirrorshades: The Cyberpunk Anthology*. Westminster, MD: Arbor House. pp. ix-xv.

Sterling, Bruce. (1989). Catscan: Slipstream. *Science Fiction Eye* 1.5, pp. 77-80.

Sterling, Bruce. (1992). *The Hacker Crackdown: Law and Disorder on the Electronic Frontier*. New York: Bantam.

Stichbury, Peter. (2014). *Anatomy of a Phenomenon*. New York: Tracy Williams, Ltd.

Tate, Greg. (1988, November 22). Diary of a Bug. *Village Voice*. p. 73.

Tate, Greg. (1992). *Flyboy in the Buttermilk: Essays on Contemporary America*. New York: Fireside.

Tate, Greg (2003a). *Midnight Lightning: Jimi Hendrix and the Black Experience*. Chicago: Lawrence Hill Books.

Tate, Greg (2003b). *Everything But the Burden: What White People are Taking from Black Culture*. New York: Harlem Moon/ Broadway.

Tate, Greg. (2004, April). Rammellzee: The Ikonoklast Samurai. *The Wire*.

Tate, Greg. (2016). *Flyboy 2: A Greg Tate Reader*. Durham, NC: Duke University Press.

Téllez, M. Eighteen. (2016). *Cyborg Memoirs*. Philadelphia, PA: DHD Heavy Industries.

Thompson, Stephen Lester. (2005). Knowwhatumsayin'? How Hip-hop Lyrics Mean. In Derrick Darby & Tommie Shelby (Eds.), *Hip-Hop and Philosophy: Rhyme 2 Reason*. Chicago: Open Court. pp. 90-98.

Tomas, Andrew. (1971). *We Are Not the First: Riddles of Ancient Science*. New York: Bantam.

Tompkins, Dave. (2010). *How to Wreck a Nice Beach: The Vocoder from World War II to Hip-Hop*. Brooklyn. NY: Melville House.

Tompkins, Dave. (2012, April 18). Period Piece: Rammellzee and the End. *The Paris Review*. Retrieved on January 17, 2015 from https://www.theparisreview.org/blog/2012/04/18/period-piece-rammellzee-and-the-end/

Tompkins, Dave. (2013). Rammellzee. In Ralph Rugoff (Ed.), *The Alternative Guide to the Universe*. London: Hayward Publishing. pp. 124-127.

Toogood, Paul & Ice-T. (2012). *Something from Nothing: The Art of Rap*. [DVD]. Directed by Ice-T & Andy Baybutt. Universal City, CA: Distributed by Vivendi Entertainment.

Toop, David. (1995). *Ocean of Sound: Aether Talk, Ambient Sound and Imaginary Worlds*. London: Serpent's Tail.

Toop, David. (1999). *Rap Attack #3: African Rap to Global Hip-Hop*. London: Serpent's Tail.

Toop, David. (2004). *Haunted Weather: Music, Silence and Memory*. London: Serpent's Tail.

Torlasco, Domietta. (2013). *The Heretical Archive: Digital Memory at the End of Film*. Minneapolis, MN: University of Minnesota Press.

Tricky. (1995). *Maxinquaye* [LP]. New York: Island Records.

Turner, Fred. (2006). *From Counterculture to Cyberculture*. Chicago: University of Chicago Press.

Tweedy, Jeff. (2004). "Theologians" [Recorded by Wilco]. On *A Ghost is Born* [LP]. New York: Nonesuch.

Uchill, Joe. (2015, November 16). How to Hide Your Digital Trail in Plain Sight. *Passcode*. Retrieved on November 18, 2015 from https://www.csmonitor.com/World/Passcode/2015/1116/How-to-hide-your-digital-trail-in-plain-sight

Urban, Greg. (2001). *Metaculture: How Culture Moves Through the World*. Minneapolis, MN: University of Minnesota Press.

Vaidhyanathan, Siva. (2001). *Copyrights and Copywrongs*: The Rise of Intellectual Property and How It Threatens Creativity. New York: NYU Press.

Vail, Mark. (2006). The "Integrative" Rhetoric of Martin Luther King Jr.'s "I Have a Dream" Speech. *Rhetoric & Public Affairs*, Vol. 9, No. 1, pp. 51-78.

Van Bakel, Rogier. (1995, June). Remembering Johnny: William Gibson on the Making of *Johnny Mnemonic. WIRED*. Retrieved on January 17, 2016 from https://www.wired.com/1995/06/gibson-4/

Van Halen. (1978). "Atomic Punk." On *Van Halen* [LP]. New York: Warner Bros.

Vitanza, Victor J. (1996). *CyberReader*. Needham Heights, MA: Allyn & Bacon.

Vold, George B. (1958). *Theoretical Criminology*. New York: Oxford University Press.

Von Däniken, Erich. (1968). *Chariots of the Gods? Unsolved Mysteries of the Past*. New York: Bantam.

Von Däniken, Erich. (1970). *Gods from Outer Space*. New York: Bantam.

Von Däniken, Erich. (1972). *The Gold of the Gods*. New York: Putnam.

Waldby, Catherine. (2002). The Instruments of Life: Frankenstein and Cyberculture. In Darren Tofts, Annemarie Jonson, & Alessio Cavallaro (Eds.), *Prefiguring Cyberculture: An Intellectual History*. Cambridge, MA: MIT Press.

Wallen, Amy. (2015, December). The Reincarnation of the Gothic into Literary Nonfiction. *The Writer's Chronicle*. (Issue, 48, #3), pp. 90-98.

Wallmark, Zachary. (2008). Grandmaster Flash. In *Musicians and Composers of the 20th Century*. Pasadena: Salem Press, pp. 531–533.

Wang, Oliver. (2006). Trapped in between the Lines: The Aesthetics of Hip-Hop Journalism. In Jeff Chang (Ed.), *Total Chaos: The Art and Aesthetics of Hip-hop*. New York: Basic Civitas, pp. 165-187.

Wark, McKenzie. (2002). *Dispositions*. Cambridge: Salt Publishing.

Wark, McKenzie (2004). *A Hacker Manifesto*. Cambridge, MA: Harvard University Press.

Warren Zanes, R. J. (1999). Too Much Mead? Under the Influence of Participant-Observation). In Kevin H. Dettmar & William Richey (Eds.), *Reading Rock and Roll: Authenticity, Appropriation, Aesthetics*. New York: Columbia University Press, pp. 37-71.

Wayner, Peter. (2009). *Disappearing Cryptography: Information Hiding: Steganography and Watermarking*. Burlington, MA: Morgan Kaufmann.

Weheliye, Alexander G. (2005). *Phonographies: Grooves in Sonic Afro-Modernity*. Durham, NC: Duke University Press.

Weheliye, Alexander G. (2014). *Habeas Viscus: Racializing Assemblages, Biopolitics, and Black Feminist Theories of the Human*. Durham, NC: Duke University Press.

Weick, Karl E., & Roberts, Karlene H. (1993). Collective Mind in Organizations: Heedful Interrelating on Flight Decks. *Administrative Science Quarterly*, 38, pp. 357–381.

Weiners, Brad. (2018, June). The Art of Disruption. *The Red Bulletin*, pp. 26-35.

Wershier-Henry, Darren. (1995). O.G. Style: Ice-T/Jacques Derrida: A Carousel CD Recording (AAD) Remixed by Darren Wershier-Henry for *Postmodern Apocalypse*. In Richard Dellamora (Ed.), *Postmodern Apocalypse: Theory and Cultural Practice at the End*. Philadelphia, PA: University of Pennsylvania Press. pp. 241-261.

West, Kanye. (2005). "Heard 'Em Say" (featuring Adam Levine) [Kanye West] from *Late Registration*. New York: Roc-A-Fella/Def Jam.

West-Pavlov, Russell. (2013). *Temporalities: The New Critical Idiom*. New York: Routledge.

Westhoff, Ben. (2016). *Original Gangstas: The Untold Story of Dr. Dre, Eazy-E, Ice Cube, Tupac Shakur, and the Birth of West Coast Rap*. New York: Hachette.

Williams, Justin A. (2013). *Rhymin' and Stealin': Musical Borrowing in Hip-hop*. Ann Arbor: MI: University of Michigan Press.

Williams, Saul. (2006). *The Dead Emcee Scrolls: The Lost Teachings of Hip-Hop*. New York: Pocket Books.

Witten, Andrew "Zephyr" & White, Michael. (2001). *Dondi White, Style Master General: The Life of Graffiti Artist Dondi White*. New York: Regan Books.

Womack, Ytasha L. (2013). *Afrofuturism: The World of Black Sci-Fi and Fantasy Culture*. Chicago, IL: Lawrence Hill.

Womack, Ytasha L. (2016). Thoughts on Navigating the Time Warp of Horrors and Riding the DNA Strands of Resilience. In *Black Quantum Futurism: Space-Time Collapse I: From the Congo to the Carolinas*. Philadelphia, PA: Afrofuturist Affair, pp. 55-64.

Woolley, Benjamin. (1992). *Virtual Worlds: A Journey in Hype and Hyperreality*. New York: Penguin.

Wu-Tang Clan. (1997). "Triumph." On *Wu-Tang Forever* [LP]. New York: Loud Records.

Young, Elizabeth. (2008). *Black Frankenstein: The Making of an American Metaphor*. New York: New York University Press.

Young, Kevin. (2012). *The Grey Album: On the Blackness of Blackness*. Minneapolis, MN: Graywolf Press.

Yu, Charles. (2010). *How to Live Safely in a Science Fictional Universe*. New York: Pantheon.

Zadeh, Joe. (2015, July 27). We Spoke to the Creator of the Chief Keef Hologram That Was Banned from Performing in Illinois. *Noisey*. Retrieved on July 8, 2018 from https://noisey.vice.com/en_us/article/6vg3vj/the-police-shut-down-the-chief-keef-hologram-so-we-talked-to-its-maker

Zuberi, Nabeel. (2001). *Sounds English: Transnational Popular Music*. Chicago: University of Illinois Press.

# CREDITS

Parts of my chapter, "The End of an Aura: Nostalgia, Memory, and the Haunting of Hip-Hop," in *The Routledge Companion of Remix Studies* (Routledge, 2015) were reworked and expanded in various places throughout *Dead Precedents*. Parts of my review of André Sirois' book *Hip-Hop DJs and the Evolution of Technology* (Peter Lang, 2016) for *The Journal of Hip-Hop Studies* (issue 4.1) are in Chapter Two, "Margin Prophets." A few ideas from my dissertation, "Allusions of Grandeur: Figurative Language Use in Rap Lyrics," appear in Chapter Four, "Spoken Windows."

All images used by kind permission of their creators:

- Afrika Bambaataa collage © Paul Insect, created for the DJ Shadow & Cut Chemist *Renegades of Rhythm* tour program.
- Chuck D collage © Ian Wright.
- Ras Kass photo © Brian Cross for Mochilla.com.
- Tricky, Rammellzee, and Danny Brown photos © Timothy Saccenti.
- Shabazz Palaces photo © Victoria Kovios. Courtesy of Sub Pop.
- Shabazz Palaces' *Quazarz: Born on a Gangster Star* cover illustration by Isvold Klincels. Design by I Want You Studio. Courtesy of Sub Pop.
- Tupac Shakur hologram photo by Eric Smith-Gunn.
- Chief Keef photo by Mary Beeze.
- Grandmaster Flash image © Gary Williams.

# ACKNOWLEDGEMENTS

While writing this book, I was often outreaching my own knowledge. So, I give special thanks to the following: To my guides in alien territory: Charles Mudede, Kodwo Eshun, Greg Tate, Ish Butler, Juice Aleem, Omar Akbar, Will Brooks, M. Sayyid, Chuck D, Steven Shaviro, Mark Dery, Hannah Liley; To the early readers of this material in various forms: Ytasha L. Womack, Samuel R. Delany, Matt Schulte, Steve Jones, Michael Schandorf, Eduardo Navas, Timothy Baker, Brian McFarland, Doug Rushkoff, Mike Daily, Andrew J. Rausch; To my fellow travelers: Dave Tompkins, Paul Edwards, Brian Coleman, Mark Katz, Simon Reynolds, Dan Charnas, André Sirois, Alex Burns, Travis Terrell Harris, Tricia Rose, Alondra Nelson, Mankwe Ndosi, Mike Ladd, Ian Bavitz, Robert Sonic Smith, Jeff Chang, Adam Bradley, David Toop, John Morrison, Alap Momin, Mike Manteca; To the artists and photographers who lent their images: Tim Saccenti, Paul Insect, Brian Cross, Ian Wright, Mary Beeze, Eric Smith-Gunn; To my dissertation committee at the University of Texas in Austin: Barry Brummett, Josh Gunn, Matt McGlone, Diane Davis, and Jeffrey Sconce; To the homies all over: You know who you are; To Stacey Spencer for stealing the only copy of *Newsweek* I've ever owned; To Thomas Durdin for expertly guiding my early hip-hop exposure.

I have been very fortunate to work with the folks at Repeater Books: Johnny Bull, Josh Turner, Jonathan Maunder, and especially Tariq Goddard. This book was much improved by their patience and diligence, as well as Tariq's sense of content, style, and humor.

All of my family who've heard me yammering about rap lyrics and UFOs for years deserve special thanks. Most especially, I have to thank my partner in all things, Lily Brewer. For some reason she listens to me talk incessantly about my dumb stuff. I owe more to her patience and attention than anything. I cannot even say.

This book is dedicated to the memories of Hsi-Chang Lin, Mark Fisher, and Sean Price. Chang was a turntablist and composer who, under the name Still, served as dälek's DJ from 2002-2005. Those guys tour relentlessly, and during that time, they always stayed at my house when they were in town. Chang and I would stay up late, talking about nothing and everything. He was a mind-blowing musician and a good friend... Mark Fisher co-founded Repeater Books. He was quick to answer when I asked for help, and his writing is of a caliber I can only aspire to... Sean Price was my favorite emcee. He taught me that you can make serious art, be serious about your craft, and still not take yourself too seriously. As he once rapped, "You do what you can, and I do what I want to." ... They are all three sorely missed.

*"To the makers of music — all worlds, all times."*

# **Repeater Books**

is dedicated to the creation of a new reality. The landscape of twenty-first-century arts and letters is faded and inert, riven by fashionable cynicism, egotistical self-reference and a nostalgia for the recent past. Repeater intends to add its voice to those movements that wish to enter history and assert control over its currents, gathering together scattered and isolated voices with those who have already called for an escape from Capitalist Realism. Our desire is to publish in every sphere and genre, combining vigorous dissent and a pragmatic willingness to succeed where messianic abstraction and quiescent co-option have stalled: abstention is not an option: we are alive and we don't agree.